Virtual Chaos

*Our Vulnerability to
Cyber-Crime and
How to Prevent It*

By
Shawn Rohrbach

ISBN: 0-9845801-4-X
ISBN-13: 978-0-9845801-4-9
Library of Congress Control Number: 2011902118

First Published by *AuthorMike Ink*, 06/18/2011

www.AuthorMikeInk.com

AuthorMike Ink and its logo are trademarked by *AuthorMike Ink Publishing*.

Printed in the United States of America

Also by
Shawn Rohrbach

Cast the First Stone
Open Your Heart with Bicycling
Strays and Other Stories
Playing the Game
Best Bike Rides in San Diego

Table of Contents

Part II – Internet Safety

Section I How the Internet Works

Section II Potential Risks of Internet Use

Section III Strategies for Safe Internet Use

Preface: A Thief's Paradise

Petty criminals, who used to resort to picking pockets, can now raid tens of thousands of bank accounts almost without detection. Gossips who once listened through walls can now "sniff" instant-message chat sessions at will for $19.95. I can check out the snow conditions at my local ski resort in seconds, and the owner of the area can no longer exaggerate them. We can continually function better, faster, and easier using the computer. Unfortunately, the same applies to criminals.

We need to open our eyes to what is coming. Cell phones, Bluetooth technologies, pacemakers, electronic ankle bracelets, and other electronic objects are already being easily tracked. Internet protocol successor IPv6 allows trillions of objects to connect to what will become a faster, more robust Internet. Imagine a time when every electronic device will be tracked and able to communicate with Internet-based applications. The prospects excite me—and, at the same time, require that I carefully study the security implications.

The computer is not going away and—with a few exceptions—those of us who have them would not voluntarily give them up. In addition to the security concerns I will raise throughout this book, an examination of a shift in our ethical behavior and consideration for how we impact the wellbeing of others through the use of computers needs to occur.

Prior to the age of easy networking, I began working with computers, sending my first email in 1979. Because there were so few available—the cost of computers being prohibitive to the average consumer—there was little fear of the kinds of security risks to be discussed in this book. As networking of computers became common, concern grew. In my first administrative position involving networking computers, our biggest fear was unskilled or fearful users who would not easily adapt to networked systems and make colossal mistakes, such as deleting data and even complete programs, accidentally. With the explosion of access to the Internet in the mid-1990s, we were introduced to an entirely new situation: people who knew computers well enough to perpetrate crimes using them.

Information technology (IT) professionals discovered early on that while some networks that were accessible from outside the organization were under attack from complete strangers, the vast majority of malicious acts were perpetrated by people inside the organization. This type of cyber crime is still the most common. As a network administrator, my attitude shifted from analyzing *if* someone had illegally intruded into various areas of my network to predicting *when* someone would try.

A common myth is that bands of disgruntled former government employees and wise (but socially inept) teenagers are the primary offenders. In fact, it is believed that this is currently the most important security risk we face. At best, these groups represent 10 percent of the risk you expose yourself to every time you boot your computer.

There are greater and more common—and in some cases unexpected—risks.

Illicit and illegal use of network resources is a costly risk. Consider the fate of an IT administrator for a very large East Coast university. As the primary administrator of information systems, he was aware of the flagrant use of the network to download and sell illegal copies of popular software programs. He served time in a federal prison because he didn't prevent the activity; in fact, he benefited financially from it.

In 2005, many businesses in the Gulf Coast area affected by Hurricane Katrina were not flooded. Even so, some small businesses were not operational because there was no electricity to operate their computers. In most areas of the southern Delta, this problem persisted for weeks or months. Companies that were lucky enough to avoid the flooding still lost money and could not access essential data. The value of secure, off-site data storage is clear in such disastrous situations.

In 2001, following the September 11th attacks, several affected companies could resume operations the following week because of astute planning. These plans included backup of all data and redundant systems deployed in obscure locations, which allowed them to relocate personnel, restore data, establish and test telecommunications, and resume business. Those who had not planned for catastrophe or potential mitigation needed months or even years to restore operations completely.

There are hundreds of very large wide area networks (WANs) that support the likes of Proctor & Gamble, Microsoft, Exxon, GM, General Electric, and

Bank of America. There are also large networks serving major universities and, through Internet2, these are further inter-networked. However, there are thousands of smaller, but equally important, computer networks supporting the majority of small home-based and business networks. These are the most vulnerable. Security issues within a small computing environment—whether at home, church, or in a small business—are equally important. Even people who know us well can be easily tempted to steal or manipulate data for a host of reasons. Risks are everywhere for those not savvy enough to recognize trouble. Consider the true story of a family-run, small, client-based business. They hired friends to work in their offices and immediately began to see client data disappearing. A close friend of 40 years was selling this data to a competitor.

Virtual Chaos: Our Vulnerability to Cyber-Crime and How to Prevent It will teach you the common risks, help you develop systems and policies for analyzing the potential for any given risk, and instruct you on taking specific, practical action to prevent and mitigate the risks. To cover this subject properly, you will need to study both the underlying technologies as well as the practical methods for securing small networks.

I will focus here on two levels of network security from the very basic principles and methods right through advanced concepts, including hardening operating systems, applying encryption, and designing redundant systems. For each topic presented, there is a theoretical explanation of the underlying technologies and the potential vulnerabilities followed by advice on mitigating or preventing any risk.

It is my firm belief that anyone who owns and operates a computer connected to the Internet can safely secure his or her systems and data. It is also my desire to convince all computer owners to begin securing their computers immediately.

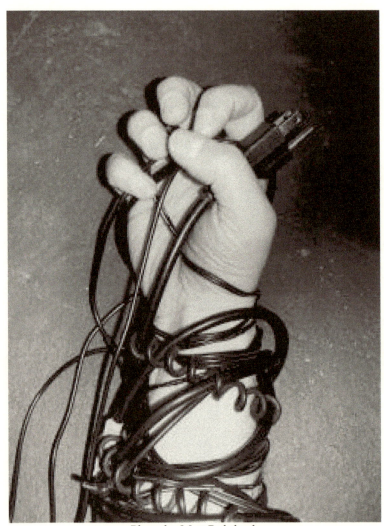
Photo by Matt Rohrbach

Part I
Fundamentals of Network Security

Section I
Network Technologies and the
Common Risks

Chapter 1: Who and What Is at Risk?

Fully understanding what the most common risks are requires focusing first on what is at risk. Too often, potential targets are overlooked until it is too late. Computer users typically only concern themselves with one or two types of potential loss. However, there are, in fact, four basic categories:

1. **Physical Security**: This type of loss could result in death or physical harm to human beings or destruction of company assets.
2. **Connectivity:** A loss of connectivity between networks can suspend normal operations.
3. **Hardware Infrastructure**: This type of loss occurs when the equipment that supports the information system fails, which can happen for any number of reasons.
4. **Data**: Data loss can suspend operations, reveal personal and financial information, and result in the loss of intellectual property.

This chapter will analyze specifically these categories of loss and how loss affects individuals and businesses.

PHYSICAL SECURITY

Threats to human life as a result of intentional or accidental failure of computer systems are rare, but they occur frequently enough to be a concern of any network security analyst. Other than possibly causing eventual degradation of eyesight or carpel-tunnel syndrome, computer systems do not directly threaten human life. The threats are typically a consequence of the actual system failure. Nevertheless, they are real.

For example, in my own area last year, a convict escaped from a local jail. He immediately sought those persons who had testified against him with the intention of murdering them. An astute police officer was successful in identifying the convict, who was recaptured before he could inflict harm. Afterward, in analyzing circumstances surrounding the jail break, it was determined that the software used to automate the prison's locks had failed, providing the convict with an opportunity to walk out the back service entrance of the jail.

In another instance, in September 2004, the computers in the air-traffic control system serving mostly California—but directly affecting the entire West Coast—failed. As a result, there was no automated air traffic control available for the West Coast for several hours, and the potential danger of commercial jets attempting to use the same air space or runways was very real. The failure was within the computerized system and directly affected the welfare of many people.

Similarly, in May 2005, the computerized tram system in Manchester, England, suffered a system-wide software failure. As the drivers had no way of piloting the trams safely, there was a complete cessation of the service due to concern for the safety of passengers.

In another scenario, a father with nefarious intentions was able to locate the day care center his child was enrolled at using the Internet. A careless web developer had allowed photographs of children on a field trip to be published online. After some searching, the father found the site and was able to then track his child's movements. He abducted his son in spite of the mother's best efforts to keep the location of the day care secret.

Systems that are computerized and designed to protect human life are rarely monitored as closely as systems housing mission-critical data. Information about ordinary people is often directly accessible over the Internet. Later in this book, systems and policies that will mitigate this risk will be introduced. The primary concern of any security plan will be to protect human life.

CONNECTIVITY

Students of information technology are often confronted with a confusing array of definitions for quality of service (QoS). Some network engineers define it as the percentage of time their server operates without requiring a reboot, which is one very small aspect of the concept of QoS. More precisely, QoS refers to the quality of the connectivity a system has with other networked systems, or the Internet in general, as well as how the data that needs to migrate is queued. QoS is comprised of both the connectivity and the hierarchy of data that then ensures the proper transfer. The primary concern is the connection. Without connectivity between systems or to the Internet, data cannot be moved.

Not every disruption of connectivity is a threat to normal operations; Internet service providers (ISP) disrupt their own service from time to time for system maintenance and upgrades. Some providers do a better job than others do of informing customers of the outages. Sometimes the customer just has to understand that his or her Internet connection is down and will come back up when the provider finishes the task or finds the failed link in the system.

Malicious disruption of Internet connectivity is not as common as technical failures; however, it does occur frequently enough to be a major concern. Worm viruses are written specifically to disrupt Internet connectivity by flooding servers and workstations until they cannot function, thereby causing connectivity to be lost.

Worse than this, however, is the student in Denver who accessed the ceiling above a server room and simply cut the network cable. The local phone company, ISP, and school network administrators scratched their heads for a while until tracing the cable to the cut by testing the cable physically. The company who originally ran the cable for the school was immediately called in to run a new cable. Internet service for the school was reestablished the next day and the student who cut the cable was never caught.

More common than malicious disruption of connectivity is disruption as a result of old or incompatible connection hardware. The relationship between national ISPs and local telecom companies in an era of deregulation is often a complex one. Frequently, the person sitting at his or her computer is prevented from contacting the local telecom company, and any problems with local connections must be dealt with through the ISP. This can result in very frustrating service calls where the local telecom technicians will test continuity of a line, but do not run data tests through sometimes-arcane connections. With the rise of a fast and secure protocol for transferring sensitive data, local telecoms are finding that their equipment was neither designed to recognize nor handle these protocols. The result is termed a *circuit flap*: data is transmitted through the local connection and as the equipment analyzes the protocols and does not recognize them, the circuit fails and the connection is lost.

Other than old equipment not recognizing new protocols, another cause in the disruption of connectivity can be in the routing tables at either end of the wide area network (WAN). Data is routed by IP and media access control (MAC) addressing. If two different people set up the routers, it is not uncommon for them to be configured differently. This will result in something that appears similar to a circuit flap, but the result is the same: loss of connectivity. Troubleshooting this type of failure requires more than simple circuit tests. Continuity can be established and maintained; yet, it will appear that there is no connectivity. More complex tests must be run to analyze the packets and frames going through the local and national telecom connections.

Later in this book, policies and methods will be discussed that will mitigate and respond to loss of connectivity. It's not your plain old telephone system (POTS) anymore. To effect these policies and mitigation plans properly, it is necessary to spend time learning about the relationship your ISP has with the local telecom companies that serve your local or national WANs.

HARDWARE INFRASTRUCTURE

It is not easy—but also not impossible—for hardware infrastructure to suffer an external attack from outside your company's walls. Examples of hardware failure fall into three categories: mechanical failure, failure caused by human intervention, and failure caused by environmental hazards.

Mechanical Failures

Hard drives, motherboards, power supplies, UPS systems, CD-ROM drives, and flash memory will all fail eventually. Hard drives on servers are as prone to failure as any home system. In fact, when various computer makers experimented with "hot swap"—the ability to pull and replace hard drives, memory, and SCSI cards while the computer is running—more hardware failure was caused.

Data can be recovered from any hard drive that fails mechanically, but not easily or cheaply. Good forensics specialists can dig hard drives out of swamps, completely dismantled, and still recover data. However, once a system fails for any of the causes listed previously, the system is nonfunctional until the hardware is replaced or repaired.

This sounds obvious and even suggests obvious solutions for mitigation, such as buying redundant hardware that can quickly replace the failed systems. However, it is not always easy to convince decision makers within a company of the necessity of redundant hardware, particularly when they have just spent a significant portion of their budget on a new server.

It is difficult to predict normal mechanical failure. Some users brag about hardware lasting almost a decade, while others see their laptops in the shop most of the time. What cannot be avoided are these two truths: hardware will fail eventually, and the computer network is most likely nonfunctional until the hardware is replaced.

Failure Caused by Human Intervention

Hardware failure caused by human intervention—whether by simple negligence or intentional malice—is far more common than simple mechanical failure. In fact, intentional damage to hardware by an internal perpetrator is exceedingly common.

For instance, in one proprietary school where I consulted, the outgoing systems administrator unwisely became close to two technical students. Once they had access to the server room, these disgruntled students poured water into the servers, routers, and switches, causing $10,000 worth of hardware and countless dollars' worth of lost productivity.

Equally destructive, and more easily preventable, are hardware failures caused by accidents involving food and beverages. I was the network administrator in a small multimedia company and, over a period of one year, I replaced 20 keyboards, 5 motherboards, and 10 power supplies as a result of employees enjoying coffee, snacks, lunch, late-night pizza, and beer at their workstations.

Hardware Failure Caused by Environmental Hazards

The loss of computer and network services due to environmental hazards is common and is not limited to catastrophic events such as earthquakes, hurricanes, floods, and fires. Dust, heat, fire prevention, improper loading of shelves and computer racks, and simple carelessness also present hazards. For instance, a server room without proper ventilation can cause hardware and, subsequently, complete system failure.

Environmental Catastrophes

In large catastrophic events where there is the risk or actual loss of human life, the primary focus is on protecting and recovering those people directly affected by the circumstances. Computer systems are quite correctly not of any concern until this task is completed. However, there are strategies for mitigating damage to computer systems; part of each mitigation plan should be rapid recovery and restoration of all information systems.

When the dust settled after the 9/11 attacks, companies assessed the damage to their information system infrastructures. No one could salvage hard drives or backup tapes due to the amount of destruction; in fact, only information backed up and stored off-site was recoverable.

Similarly, during and after Hurricane Katrina, rescuers could not devote their energies to recovering hard drives, backup tapes, or computer systems. Whole systems serving banks, insurance companies, schools, and hospitals were completely inoperable. If the systems were not backed up prior to the storm and flooding, the data was lost.

In Indonesia, villages had struggled for years to build computing services, only to see them wiped out completely by the tsunami of December 2004. Long after the event, villages that were able to rebuild still have not replaced their computing systems.

Minor Catastrophic Phenomena

The heat generated by servers not properly ventilated can cause catastrophic system failure. With prolonged exposure to heat, system boards will often fail. While an overheated room is not viewed as the most important threat to a networking system, more time is spent by network administrators mitigating or repairing network problems because of this seemingly insignificant issue.

DATA

Data can be lost, destroyed, or stolen. Sensitive data containing trade secrets, operational information, and personal records can be used for financial gain or simply to destroy someone's life or business. This is particularly important in an environment that handles sensitive defense or government information. Chapter 12 will focus specifically on how compliance to NISP standards helps network administrators protect student privacy and the integrity of their data.

There are a variety of methods for gaining access to data. It is common to think that data is most vulnerable to hackers who access systems remotely and steal or destroy. The truth is that most networks are fairly well protected at the perimeter using a variety of routing techniques, firewalls, and fireboxes within a secure architecture. In fact, it has been clearly proven that internal personnel usually cause data to be lost, stolen, or destroyed, either accidentally or maliciously. A terrorist will have better luck stealing data if he or she has a job within the company that he or she wants to steal from.

As an experiment, I once parked outside the office of a large regional bank with a laptop outfitted with inexpensive software used to "sniff" chat sessions. Most instant messaging services use the same protocols and the same ports. Data in the chat sessions migrates across the wired or wireless network as plain text. In simple terms, anyone with $40 worth of chat-sniffing software can easily intercept chats that are taking place on any given network.

I had warned the managers of this bank that I knew of people who had intercepted their chats, and quite by accident. They did not express much concern; that is, until I handed them a printout of five chat sessions taking place between employees and customers with regard to commercial loans. The printouts contained extremely private information, including phone numbers, social security numbers, bank account information, and more. The managers immediately directed employees to stop using all forms of instant messaging until they could encrypt the data and formulate new policies that would ensure the safe use of this communication tool.

Sniffing chats is not the only problem with most instant messaging services. The protocol most typically used, H.323, allows sessions to remain opened on the default port. Two people may be in a session, but are not typing information. The ports on both ends are in a receptive mode and are not shielded from receiving any kind of data, especially viruses and spyware. Rather than bothering to encrypt data and secure ports, most corporate IT personnel simply request policies forbidding the use of instant messaging.

A network administrator for a large, multi-location corporation was mandated to conduct regular backups and to have those backup tapes stored securely off-site. The corporation retained the services of a company that routinely picked up data storage tapes and stored them in underground vaults. The driver for the data storage company, who was required to report the number of tapes picked up at each location, wasn't reporting on the client company. An auditor was sent to review the log books and to visit the network administrator. The auditor found 900 backup tapes in boxes in the basement of the facility. A rainstorm had caused the drainage to overflow and most of the tapes had been submerged under water until the drain was cleared, destroying all the data.

Now that we know what can be lost, let's look at the basic technologies of computer networking so that we can understand why there are these risks and begin to plan properly for security.

Chapter 2: How Computers Really Work and What Makes Them Vulnerable

In spite of many attempts by computer specialists to complicate information technology, it is actually easy to understand. For the purposes of this book, we will focus on how data—whether email, Word documents, photographs, or video—is created, transmitted, and viewed. This will help us to understand the subsequent issues pertaining to network security.

Let's start with the creation of data. Computer programs are designed to make it easy to write a letter. We see the actual document, photograph, or video as the recipient will see it. However, for the data to be stored or transmitted it must be converted to something that low-voltage electricity can handle. The result is binary code, using only the digits 1 or 0.

Hard drives in computers or fancy flash drives people carry around can only see these patterns of ones and zeros. Computer programs, when instructed, search for specific patterns and either reproduce them on the monitor or send them to the printer so that we have a hard copy of what was once nothing more than electronic impulses.

Every letter in the alphabet, number, and symbol on a computer keyboard has a specific pattern of ones and zeros. Each 1 or 0 is a *bit*, and eight of these in a specific pattern are called a *byte*. The word *dog* has 24 bits, or 3 bytes, each 1 or 0 in the byte pattern represents the letters *D*, *O*, and *G*. A word-processing software program will read these patterns and produce the word *dog* on the screen.

Old-school programmers once wrote software applications using binary code. They had memorized roughly 250 different binary representations of letters, numbers, and symbols. Subsequent programmers were given tools to program, called *compilers*. They could write programs in a way that represented their speaking language and the compiler would convert this to binary and store it on the hard drive. If someone takes a digital picture at a birthday party, it is always coded in patterns of ones or zeros until either viewed on the screen or sent to a printer to become a hard-copy photograph.

The basis of all computer networking is:

1. Data is converted from common language or visual representation to binary code, or patterns of ones and zeros.
2. These ones and zeros are transmitted using low-voltage electricity.
3. The code is reassembled at the recipient's computer for viewing, printing, or storage.

Low-voltage electricity can pass through a wide variety of mediums. Typically, it passes through thin copper wire, such as telephone wire or what is known as Cat 5, a wire typically used for computer networks. Low-voltage electricity can also pass through glass tubes (commonly known as fiber optics), copper pipes, barbed wire, and anything else that allows conductivity.

Data, or electronic impulses that are read as on or off (ones or zeros), can safely pass through anything that allows conductivity. This is always a concern for network security personnel; data that is passing with low-voltage electricity can pass through almost anything and can also be easily diverted or viewed as it passes. If a word-processing program created the document, the same word-processing program can open the document and read it. Therefore, the document can also be opened and read by other programs. This is the first concern in computer network security.

The next concept to understand is how data is distributed. Computer networking was developed to deliver data accurately. There is nothing useful about a system that delivers inaccurate or partial data. All the data must be reproduced by another computer exactly the way the writer or photographer intended for it to be seen.

Low-voltage electricity passing through copper wire can carry only small amounts of data at any given time, about one page of written material. Fiber optic and cable wires can carry slightly larger amounts of data in one segment. Let's say I want to send my most recent mystery novel to an unsuspecting editor who will be thrilled to receive it in his morning email. My novel is 1,300 pages long and has a surprise ending. I need to break this novel down into about 1,300 different segments of ones and zeros, and then have it reassemble as the editor anxiously opens his email and finds my delightful novel.

Computer programs know this and are written to divide data into packets or frames. The mechanism that is used to organize the packets or frames so that they reassemble correctly at the recipient computer is important. Each packet is tagged with a number so that the 1,300 packets of my novel reassemble correctly, and I have a better chance of getting a contract on my book. The packet also carries two other types of information to ensure that my novel arrives at the editor's desk and not my archrival novelist's, who wants to steal my ideas.

This system was developed by several different scientists and was partially funded by the defense department, who wanted a computerized system for tasks such as sending commands to nuclear weapons. The system was designed to be accurate. The command would be sent from one point to another exact point, such as a missile silo. Sending the command to every computer in the world and hoping the right computer would read it was completely unacceptable. The additional data is an addressing system that identifies the network the computer is on as well as the exact computers that are the sender and the recipient. It is the same concept as snail mail; write the correct address on the envelope and the letter will probably arrive at the correct address.

The first address is an Internet protocol (IP) address and the second is a media access control (MAC) address.

- The IP address identifies the network and locates the computer.
- The MAC address specifically identifies the computer.

For those of you reading and wondering how law enforcement knows who is sending what data, especially illegal data, this framework is the basis of that investigative work. These addresses might change for any number of reasons, but the history of the activity is permanently archived in computer network systems. It never goes away. I once worked for an Internet service provider ISP archiving data and addresses for email that was sent through their servers. Most of it was pure dribble, but occasionally it was taken as evidence of illegal activity on the Internet, and the history of that activity was permanently preserved. The result was a rightful conviction. The key principle is simple: Computer networks were invented to be precise, not private. This is the second important concept to understand in reference to network security.

Next, let's look at data storage. Earlier in this book, when I alluded to Hurricane Katrina, the total loss of information assets and resources was not limited to computers submerged under water. Legal, financial, and other types of data were permanently lost. Bank records reflecting savings, checking, and investment accounts were similarly gone. If there were no duplicate copies of this data in storage, these records were lost permanently.

Data is stored in binary format in various ways, on metallic hard drive disks, metallic tape, and even in glass. Of greatest concern is the integrity of the data; that is, that it is the exact data that was intended to be stored. In reference to the emails I archived for the ISP, all the data associated with those emails must be properly intact or it is not evidence.

In the same vein, when you work somewhere, the data regarding your paychecks must be exactly what was agreed upon. If you are paid too much, then you should report it and, certainly if you are paid too little, you will definitely report it. In either case, the data regarding the paycheck needs to be accurate.

Permanently destroying data is one way to corrupt it. The company can assume that you never existed and not pay you at all. Improperly entering the data can also corrupt it. Adding another zero to your salary looks good, but it's not what the company agreed to pay you. This kind of data corruption usually gets all the attention and will be handled in good time in this book.

The reality is that data is never permanently destroyed. People think that "deleting" a file really means permanently removing the file from a storage medium such as a hard or flash drive. In fact, the file is only masked and the computer is told to write data over the deleted data. The old data remains. Software applications have been developed to identify data that has been overwritten, look for patterns of ones and zeros, and then reproduce the "deleted" data. As a demonstration, I used to have my students "delete" a file, then disassemble the hard drive, throw the hard drive disks in water, and leave them over night. The next morning, I dry the disk, reassemble the hard drive, and find and display the deleted file. If I sell or recycle a computer, I remove the hard drive, remove the disk from the hard drive case, attack the disk with a hammer, and properly dispose of the shattered disk according to local law. Then the data is permanently destroyed.

Permanent destruction of data stored on a typical hard drive is difficult, but not impossible. Recovery of the data requires very expensive software. Data stored on magnetic tape is easily destroyed. The tape can easily be burned, cut, overheated, or soaked in water, and the magnetic qualities are lost along with the data. This is a primary concern when thinking of safely storing data, as well.

Data entry is a flawed process. For example, when I was in high school, the Army was convinced that I was a female and hotly recruited me to join up. Someone had simply entered my name into the arcane computer and selected "female" when they identified my sex. There is an old, well-worn expression that refers to this as GIGO: Garbage In, and Garbage Out. Even the most current scanning hardware and software make mistakes and misidentify letters, numbers, and characters, and the data is then corrupted. The computer will accept as true any keystroke you enter, no matter how badly the word or number is mangled.

Data is only as good as the method of transferring it to a digital format and the media on which it is stored. Enter the data correctly and choose a media that will survive the natural destruction caused by exposure to elements or disasters and you should be safe.

CONCLUSION

This chapter looked at the essential elements of data without getting caught up in some of the complexities of specific data processing. Computers deal with data in a manner that allows us to see the product, but always manipulates, transmits, and stores it in binary form. These ones and zeros are transmitted to exact locations using addresses and low-voltage electricity, and finally the data is stored in a somewhat permanent fashion as binary.

This may seem simplistic—and it really is. Computer networking was designed around the existing telephone infrastructure because twisted copper wire was known to efficiently conduct low-voltage electricity and then binary data. The invention of the modem—a device that converts digital low voltage to analog low voltage that can be easily transmitted over existing telephone wires—was the biggest early step in revolutionizing computer networking and it gave birth to the explosion of the Internet. The basics of computer networking have not changed even though the medium of transmission over fiber optic and cable allow for faster transmission of larger packets and frames. With this understanding of the essentials of networking technologies, we can successfully proceed to securing a computer network system.

Chapter 3: Documenting the Network

Approaching network security in a disorganized fashion will ultimately result in some form of loss. A tightly organized security plan will not guarantee prevention of all loss, but the odds are substantially better. The best security plan begins with a thorough assessment of the network as it stands. Changes can be made more easily and effectively to a system after a thorough assessment.

To complete this assessment effectively, it must be undertaken by an individual or group who is authorized to access all areas of the network. Denying access will only result in an incomplete assessment. In fact, many consultants will walk away from clients who did not give total access.

It is also advisable to complete the assessment before trying to fix anything. The only exception would be if during the assessment it was discovered that someone was actively attempting to access data illicitly or if something illegal was discovered in the process. Laws vary between jurisdictions, but generally, proof of fraudulent activity, theft, purposeful destruction of data, storage of illegal pornography, and other obviously illegal activities need to be reported immediately to local authorities. This delays the assessment, but to have total access to a system and then to ignore proof of illegal activity places some level of guilt on the assessor.

Aside from reporting illegal activity, this assessment is not intended to seek out minute problems; rather, it is intended to give administrators a thorough overview of the system. Many network administrators who were never formally trained in network architecture simply hack together working networks. I have assessed numerous networks and I've been amazed at the creative methods used to design them, often without any consideration for efficiency or optimal performance. Astute and experienced network administrators will see the obvious flaws in a badly designed system and be prepared to offer thorough remedies rather than simply patching a system on the fly. Later, an assessment of specific vulnerabilities and performance can be conducted more effectively.

A thorough assessment of a small home-based business network covers the following areas:

1. Cabling
2. Distribution hardware
3. Central processing units (CPUs)
4. Networked peripherals
5. Physical security of server and data storage devices
6. Existing policies

A more complex assessment is usually made of more elaborate systems, but for our purposes, this is usually sufficient.

CABLING

New construction often guarantees state-of-the-art cabling throughout the structure. Retrofitted office and home improvements cannot be guaranteed to work effectively. Cabling is as important as any other aspect of a network, and the security of the network relies on it as much as on anything else. Recalling the first chapter on determining what is at risk in a network, the actual connectivity and effective delivery of data depends on the quality of the cabling infrastructure.

Starting at the *demarcation point*, or where the network connection enters the building, you will want to follow or test every cable connection to the point where the node plugs in.

Demarcation

In a small network, the demarcation point can be as simple as where the cable or telephone company has their connection box on the side of the structure. Check for loose or exposed wires. Look for damage to the box used to cover the connections, illicit connections, and vampire taps. Someone with a good understanding of electronics can easily tap into a cable or telephone system to steal cable television and Internet service or to monitor the transmission of data. Connections should be clean and obvious. If anything seems out of order or there appear to be connections that are not clearly identified or are loose, call the service provider responsible for the demarcation connection.

In a larger network, the local telephone service provider, such as Verizon or Quest, usually controls the demarcation point. They control access to the lines that are rented by long distance service providers. Typically, a company with multiple locations will contract a separate national long distance service, which provides local telephone service. Long distance service providers contract with the local provider to connect your telephone, DSL, ADSL and often fiber optic.

Most business parks are not serviced by cable companies. This is significant because if there is an issue with the cabling, a company cannot normally contact the local provider unless they also provide telephone service. You must contact your long distance provider, which rents the lines, and they will contact the local company to service the demarcation point.

Now start tracing the cabling from the demarcation point to the first point of distribution, typically in the server room. If this cable is exposed, you have a problem; if the cable were cut, your facility could lose all Internet connectivity.

Once in the server room, try to determine if the cabling going to the various nodes is clearly marked. If not, you will want to make a note to remedy this later. A well-installed cable infrastructure is clearly marked at both ends of the cable in the server room and at the point in the wall where the node connects. This helps quickly identify cabling issues.

To test Cat 5 cabling, all you need is a line tester, costing no more than $75, and an inexpensive set of handheld radio transceivers. The line tester will tell if the cable and RJ45 heads were wired for straight-through or crossover throughput; typically, you want a straight-through connection. The tester will also reveal if there is line interruption such as a cut.

At this point, a diagram of the cabling infrastructure should be drawn, noting the nomenclature of the end points that match in the server room and where the nodes connect.

This diagram will be very helpful in the event of loss of service to various nodes or sections.

Cabling from the wall connection to the node should be neatly tucked out of sight, using zip ties or some other connection to secure cables together. Loose, sagging, or visible cabling running from the wall to the node is unsightly and deteriorates users' impressions of the infrastructure. If they hold the network in low regard, they will not care for it as well as they should. A neat and tidy network helps to create an environment of respect for the computer network.

DISTRIBUTION HARDWARE

In general, distribution hardware, such as multiport hubs, switches, routers, and bridges, are secured behind a locked door in the server room along with the server and other storage devices. Each manufacturer has its own specific commands or user interfaces for configuring these devices, a subject which will be discussed in more detail later in this book. These devices' specific location should be noted on the now-growing network diagram.

The diagram should show the distances between these devices and the demarcation point, as well as the longest distances from the server room to the most remote nodes on the network. It should also clearly identify the order of the distribution hardware. Note the first piece of hardware that is connected to the cable coming from the demarcation point. It could be a packet shaper, router, switch, or bridge, depending on the architecture chosen.

Note each subsequent piece of hardware in line, including the server and any other CPUs in the server room.

Make a note in the documentation of any of hardware that is not functioning properly as this may identify causes of existing problems once all the data has been collected.

CENTRAL PROCESSING UNITS

Count the CPUs that should be connected to the network; this information should be included in the documentation. Note the following, as it is useful in determining the capacity of a network, building rendering farms, understanding what software can and cannot be installed, and when auditing user activity on a network:

- Manufacturer's identifier
- Serial numbers
- MAC addresses
- Amount of installed memory
- Processor power
- Hard drive capacity
- CD-ROM or DVD drives
- USB ports
- PCI cards installed after purchase

Normally, a good administrator has a naming convention for the CPUs. One administrator might choose cartoon character names, another a number system. The names are configured in the operating system and it is easy to identify the CPU and immediately know the capacity limitations.

Knowing these details serves to speed the process of troubleshooting desktops, servers, and supporting CPUs.

Note in the documentation the software installed on each CPU and locate the licensing information for all installed software. During the assessment phase, the focus is to identify licensed and unlicensed software. Downloading and using commercial software without proper licensing is illegal; it is tantamount to stealing. If you are, or become, the administrator of the computer network, you will want all CPUs and their corresponding software to be in compliance with the law. Well-managed networks do not permit users to install their own software. This helps to keep the network in compliance.

It is important to identify if there are variations in the operating systems used and even variations in the generations of operating systems. This information is useful when trying to troubleshoot desktop issues.

NETWORKED PERIPHERALS

Printers, scanners, DVD burners, and projectors can all be managed in a network environment. Each networked item receives an IP address and possesses a MAC address. As you document the network, these nodes should also be named and located on the network diagram.

PHYSICAL SECURITY OF SERVER AND STORAGE DEVICES

Document the existing conditions of the server room. It is imperative to secure the server(s) in a locked, air-controlled room that is large enough to work in without the risk of physical damage to any hardware or cabling. In two network environments that I have worked in, the server rooms were neither locked nor air-conditioned; the temperature of the room in the summer would reach 115 degrees. There were multiple servers for a variety of functions and two of those servers were lost due to overheated motherboards.

Limit access to the server room as well, and ensure that it is not used as a storage room or a workspace. During the assessment phase, determine who has access to the room and for what purpose. There should be adequate clearance around all the servers and distribution hardware in the room. Determine how the hardware is secured to racks and if the racks can be locked.

Take notice of the location of fire-suppression systems, especially ceiling-mounted water fire-suppression systems. In the event of a fire, the safety of people comes first, but it is also possible to plan for the safety of server room hardware. Make note in the documentation of how fires would be suppressed and the proximity of the server room to outdoor safety. Local codes may require water-based fire suppression, in which case there is a very short period of time during which you can safely salvage a server. Make sure you understand how to deal with live electricity in the event that water is spraying into the server room. If you do not know how to deal with this, leave the server room and evacuate to safety.

WRITTEN POLICIES

Unfortunately, all too often the norm is the absence of effective or comprehensive policies to govern users, data security, reporting of crimes, and continuity. Begin by determining whether any policies have been written and properly adopted. The writing and implementation of these policies will be covered later in this book, but during the assessment phase, document all existing (or nonexistent) written policies. Read the policies that do exist. Note in the documentation any discrepancies between the written policies and what actually exists in the network. This will come in handy later.

Before taking on the role of network administrator, the assessment and documentation of a network should occur. It will help identify potential or existing problems as well as serve as a baseline of activity that preceded your total access to the network. The network administrator should preserve the documentation and copy it to the owner of the system. The politics of network administration are such that the new administrator's primary working relationship is with the owner of the system or the individual he or she has designated to undertake the ownership role. The administrator should not immediately trust the preceding administrator unless he or she has been instructed to do so. The assessment phase should be a clean and impartial process that is nothing more than a statement of fact.

Chapter 4: Writing and Testing Security Policies

Up to this point, we have discussed basic networking concepts and documented the existing network as it is. Usually, there are no security policies in place, especially in a home or small-business network. Even in large, complex enterprise environments, this can be the case. Security policies seem like a tedious chore until it is too late. To proceed through basic computer security and to some advanced issues, we need to know what we want to secure, how to secure it, and how this affects the actions of legitimate users. What is needed is a well-planned written security policy.

The upcoming chapters might serve as a framework for a security policy, or you may choose to combine topics or delete those that do not relate to your operations. This chapter will help you develop a written policy that will lead to a secure network.

Policies in written form do not necessarily prevent malicious attacks on a network; they need to be adopted and implemented, and they need to properly address the security issues specific to the network, as outlined in chapter 3. This documentation will detail how the network stands today without commentary or judgment. An astute administrator will already have an opinion about how secure the network environment is. Now, the work of shaping a living document that will grow with the network and provide levels of security begins.

There are many questions to ask during the policy phase that do not come up in the assessment phase. For instance:

- *Does the documentation reveal a carefully planned internal and external strategy for securing data and computing assets?*
- *Are there regular updates of virus protection and are the procedures for this clearly stated?*
- *Is there a clear policy regarding who can access certain files and are these properly implemented in the operating system?*
- *Is there a clear understanding of the possible environmental hazards in the area, and have proper mitigation procedures been put in place to minimize the effects of them?*
- *How does a new employee get a login and password, and how is that password managed? Could access to restricted files be easily gained by lifting another employee's keyboard and seeing his or her password?*
- *Can anyone access the wireless system?*
- *As the company grows, is there a plan in place that scales the network and the security at the same time?*
- *What happens if an employee or member of the family steals movies or downloads patently offensive material? Are procedures in place to properly handle this issue?*
- *Is there a regular procedure for taking highly sensitive data to secure storage?*

- *Who is the keeper of the administrative password and how widely is that password distributed?*
- *Is there a concerted effort to plan properly for the dismissal or voluntary departure of key IT personnel?*

At each new location where I work or consult, the answers to these questions are usually negative. Most organizations wing it until there is a problem. Without a clear policy—say, for viewing and downloading even legal pornography—attempts to fire the offender will probably fail. The result may be a sexual harassment lawsuit from others within the organization who are upset by the activity and the inability of the organization to stop it.

Without a complete and thoroughly tested policy, the downloading of pornographic material is a very small problem when you consider what else could happen. Further, once a policy is in place, it must be monitored for compliance and subsequently enforced. Attempting to discipline an employee using a policy that is not consistently monitored or enforced will probably fail and may result in a lawsuit being filed by the employee. These are the four basic steps toward developing an effective security policy:

1. Review potential risks and the business needs of the organization.
2. Address specific issues with specific policies.
3. Educate, advise, and then implement the policies.

4. Review and modify the policies on a regular basis.

REVIEW POTENTIAL RISKS AND THE BUSINESS NEEDS OF THE ORGANIZATION

As discussed in chapter 1, there are specific assets of a networked environment that are at risk: physical security, connectivity, hardware infrastructure, and data. It is essential now to place a value on everything that falls within these categories.

For instance, a database of customer names might regularly yield a company $3 million in sales each year. Is that the face value of the database if it was destroyed or stolen? How much could you insure the database for?

A new rack of blade servers in a data center with all distribution hardware intact might cost about $300,000. How quickly does this value depreciate once it is in place and what is its value one month, one year, and five years after implementation?

A proprietary CRM application costs $400,000 to plan, write, and implement. If someone was able to penetrate the security and ruin this application, rendering it worthless, what value does that have in replacement and loss of business?

The owner of these assets needs to decide how secure to make the network based on the value of the assets being protected. Consider this parallel: The British government spends sizeable sums of money protecting the crown jewels. Yet, a neighbor we had growing up spent absolutely no money protecting the pile of old tires he had in his backyard. Translating that to a computer network, if you have a few games and your favorite Internet links on your computer, security is not much of a worry; however, if you are holding the electronic versions of plans for futuristic weapons for the Department of Defense, you need to spend time and money on security.

I make this point because many security plans fail when a proper value assessment is not made. Similarly, if the security is either cost prohibitive or protects valueless assets, or if extremely valuable assets are permanently lost because no security was implemented, the security plan is a failure. Provide security commensurate with the value of the assets.

ADDRESS SPECIFIC ISSUES WITH SPECIFIC POLICIES

A director of a well-funded program was undoubtedly red-faced when local police were investigating the loss of a database of donors. The director had agreed to purchase an expensive firebox in addition to upgrading the routers. Everyone sat comfortably behind a well-guarded firewall. However, the data was stolen from the inside as the network administrator watched dutifully at the perimeter for intrusions. The donors might have continued to give to the program, but the issue was not so much the loss of the database as it was the revelation of the personal assets and value of the donors. Some of the information became public and an extortion attempt followed to suppress the remainder of the personal data.

In another case study, a company spent thousands of dollars on antivirus and operating-system updates, but failed to analyze the physical security of their building properly. Fifteen computers, including the servers and the data farm, were carried effortlessly out the door. The antivirus applications might have been necessary, but they could also have been excessive. The potential loss from theft was not taken into consideration. Maybe an alarm system and more durable locks would have been better purchases, followed later by the antivirus protection.

It is important to list all the potential risks and, once they have been prioritized by dollar value and importance to operations, address each in a manner consistent with their value. Security policy might include these elements as procedures for very basic antivirus updating and procedures for extensive monitoring of physical security, which would make sense in a networked environment where Internet access was not necessary. In that particular facility, there would be little or no exposure to outside viruses, but the company might be located in an area that either experiences high crime rates or where the exits are obscured with landscaping. All security threats must be addressed in the written policy.

EDUCATE, ADVISE AND THEN IMPLEMENT THE POLICY

Once all the risks have been evaluated and a proper response formulated, the policy is not going to be effective until people understand why it was written, what it hopes to attain, how it impacts their behavior, and how it will become a mandatory part of their terms of employment. You will probably need the services of a lawyer for this stage.

Most managers now know that if they do not have mandatory written policies presented and consented to in writing by each employee, then they might as well not have a policy. This is really the easy part, however; after an introduction period, employees should be required to sign an acceptance form of the new policies. There is a stated implementation date and, following that date, they must comply with the new policies. (A good lawyer will make fast business of this part.)

The difficulty in introducing security policies, even after they become mandatory, is getting people to follow them. It's preferable to have buy-in and willing participation in the policy than to have to fire someone because he or she forgot to lock the server room door. Therefore, take the time to educate your employees.

The most troublesome security breakdown is the tendency people have to write passwords in a notebook or on a slip of paper kept within arm's reach of a keyboard or to give passwords out when checking in on sick or personal days. Even with specific policies and a signed agreement in place, physical audits of workstations often reveal high percentages of employees violating this policy. Even when employees were warned of reprimand, in addition to confiscated and changed passwords, many still failed to comply with the policy.

In both private commercial and academic environments, the need to provide a clean, safe, and comfortable working environment is paramount, and this includes the viewing and downloading of immoral or offensive material. A security policy should also cover this topic and it needs to be discussed during routine sexual harassment presentations and with new hires. It is advisable to conduct comprehensive network security training during orientation. Cover all issues pertaining to employee activity and behavior that affect the network.

It's not uncommon to hear grumblings about network administrators. Security policies can be very powerful and might best be kept out of the hands of the power-hungry. The policies are intended to secure the environment, assets, and data, not to give administrators a thing to bludgeon employees with. When enforcing security policies, there has to be an iron fist inside a velvet glove. Violations of the security policy could affect operations and diminish profits. Handle these situations professionally and in compliance with local human resource laws, and be sure that the punishment fits the crime. Berating and humiliating someone for an accidental violation might serve to break down morale and inhibit people from observing policies. I have known cases where employees have turned on their companies and tried to wreak havoc on the network after inappropriate treatment during one of these episodes.

REVIEW AND MODIFY THE POLICY ON A REGULAR BASIS

As conditions change, so must the security policy. The introduction of new databases, new operating systems, new divisions within the company, and any change necessary to accommodate growth should all be integrated into the policy. For example, a company might allow employees to surf the Internet from their workstations for the first time, which would elevate the need for consistently updating antiviral protection. An outsourced company may be retained to provide desktop backup for all workstations; this would change how employees and internal administrators would deal with desktop issues.

New architectures that help achieve secure, scalable environments are emerging. Often, an organization must put aside the revered DMZ and firewall and make changes to satisfy the needs of the business. A number of administrators do not educate themselves on emerging trends; instead, they cling to old-school methodologies that might be relatively secure but diminish performance. Scaling a network to accommodate growth, but with security paramount, will be discussed later in this book.

Over time, you should test your security policies. You can allow someone on the outside to try and attack your systems, and you can plant someone on the inside to roam the hallways and gather whatever data he or she can to find any internal leaks. However, there are few companies who have staff well-trained enough to test the internal systems.

An innovation in the industry are companies that do "white hat" testing of external security. External penetration testing will require written permission by the owner of the system and the specifications must be very clear as to what the test is looking for. Most legitimate penetration tests proceed no further than the open port. Their report will make clear what they have found and what vulnerabilities exist. Typically, this kind of test should be completed without the knowledge of the network administrator. Advanced knowledge of the test would possibly allow the administrator to examine his or her own configurations ahead of time and make corrections. While this might be the desired outcome, it is always good to have a fully objective analysis of the system security.

The internal tests are a little more difficult to plan and implement, but they should include:

- Some social engineering to determine if personnel are sharing passwords
- An audit of attempts to access restricted drives or files
- A physical audit of workstations to see if passwords are easily accessible
- An audit of workstations to determine if Internet use is in compliance with company policies

I have always consulted with company attorneys before conducting this kind of internal audit. First, I want to know if the employees are aware that the owner of the company has declared in advance the possibility of this test, and that the employees have acknowledged this in writing. Without prior notice, it is always difficult to proceed with further education or disciplinary action for violations of policy. I make it a point to warn business owners that they might not like what they see during the security audit. Their most treasured employee or their sister's kid who they are helping out might turn out to be extremely careless—or even malicious—in his or her practices or attempts to manipulate data.

A good test will reveal any possible weaknesses. Furthermore, internal weaknesses might point to a need to conduct more training and education on the importance of security and the policies that define it.

Chapter 5: Reducing Environmental Hazards

I'll admit that the only time I have ever lost hardware, software, or data in my 20 years of managing computer resources was when I was writing several emails at Christmastime to catch up with friends and family, and I happened to spill a drink on my laptop keyboard. The motherboard was shot, and in those days, there were no discount electronics stores selling them for a bargain. The hard drive was corrupted, and a company gladly bid to retrieve the data. The cost of repairing the laptop and retrieving data then was prohibitively expensive and I passed. The data was stored on various media and once I could afford a new laptop, I was up and running.

I worked for several years in an academic environment that prided itself on offering current technology to its students. For the most part, the hardware was good. Most students could not afford the CPUs we had in the labs, and we refreshed those computers every six months. We had to ensure that they always operated optimally. The biggest threat we experienced in our labs was not hackers or viruses; it was a carbonated, caffeinated beverage, a favorite of gamers and people who spend long hours in front of a computer. Over seven years spent administering that network, motherboards, keyboards, CD-ROM drives, and even printers suffered due to the bumping or spilling of this soft drink. Coffee was the second biggest culprit.

In an office environment, where employees have regular access to the same workstation, food is always an issue. Sweet rolls, mayonnaise, birthday cake, you name it, I pulled or wiped it out of CPUs, keyboards, mice, scanners, printers . . . You get the idea. People are careless with food and try hard to cover up their carelessness, often blaming other people.

In February 2001, the Seattle area witnessed a fairly severe earthquake, which knocked down some brick buildings in the old part of the city. Among the ruins, sitting for several days out in the elements and under crushed brick, were numerous workstations, distribution hardware, and servers, many of which had been processing or storing extremely important data when the earthquake struck. Even if the hard drives had been intact, owners were not allowed to retrieve them until after city engineers had cleared the buildings for safety.

In the facility that I was managing, we had secured the workstations to the legs of steel desks. We were not thinking of earthquake protection when we did this; rather, because some RAM had been stolen, slowing down thieves had motivated me. I had removed the CPU cover screws and zip-tied the case to the steel legs. During the earthquake, I recalled the emergency preparedness training that advised getting under a steel desk, which would probably support the collapse of a falling ceiling. I instructed everyone in the lab to crawl under their desks. As we tumbled and shook, I noticed that the CPUs stood secure and motionless. No hardware was lost during the quake.

We can prepare for many disasters, but not all. Even if we do prepare, there is no guarantee against loss of data or computing assets. This chapter will get you pointed in the right direction. The action items that follow can also be used to help prevent theft of computing assets.

FROM THE DEMARCATION POINT TO THE SERVER ROOM

If you visually traced the media that connects the demarcation point to the server room during your assessment, you are aware of this cable's proximity to sharp objects and excessive heat, as well as if the cable is susceptible to being cut by falling objects. Determine any risk to this cable and mitigate it by eliminating the sharp objects and excessive heat or by rerunning the cable through a heat- and crush-resistant conduit.

If you can too easily see and trace this cable, do whatever you can to conceal it. An elite Seattle-area private school once suffered a complete loss of network services because of just this issue. The cable from the demarcation point to the server room was tacked to the ceiling and, in some cases, drooped down low enough for a person to touch it. In fact, someone did—with a pair of bolt cutters in five or six places.

During my own assessment of a new DSL system installed at one location, I found what is known as a "vampire tap" on the cable from demarcation to the server room. This device is used to monitor and capture data passing across the system. Unless a law enforcement agency has valid permission to install one, it is illegal. We were never able to determine who had placed the device, and the matter was turned over to the police.

AT THE SERVER ROOM

If the organization does not currently have rack-mountable hardware and a server/hardware rack that is secured to the floor and wall, plan on getting them. Loosely stacked hardware can easily fall, get kicked, or be tripped over, thereby increasing the risk of losing the hardware or connectivity. Securing hardware to a rack also will increase the possibility of limiting damage in the event of a fire.

As stated previously, check for fire-suppressant sprinkler heads and observe how easily, in the event of an emergency, it will be to safely remove the hardware and prevent water damage. I know of a handful of administrators who have successfully prevented water damage in the event that sprinklers were set off, but in every case, the alarms were false. In the case of a real fire, evacuate safely and let the fire department do their job. Servers are easily replaced; people are not.

Check the local flood tables in your area. Each county keeps statistics and records about the possibility of flooding. Some real estate developers build on flood plains or on former wetlands, where the seasonal rainwater hasn't yet been properly mitigated. Don't assume your business will never be flooded. Racking the hardware two or three feet off the ground will help prevent damage from natural flooding as well as flooding caused by broken water pipes or a leaky roof.

WORKSTATIONS

You need to make local command decisions about the most critical risks to labs and desktop workstations. For instance,

I chose to secure the workstations in my labs to the steel desk legs. I used several plastic zip ties and it took us an average of ten minutes to completely free a workstation. I decided this was an inexpensive way to slow down, and perhaps discourage, thieves; it also served as a measure of security against a major earthquake.

I was also confident enough in the general structure of the building and determined that the roof had been replaced, so leaks were not likely. If I had thought the roof was potentially a flooding source, I would have tried to create a local solution to compensate for all these potential risks. When the same area later suffered a record-setting windstorm and a large tree fell on the tilt-up concrete building, the wooden roof and the false-panel ceiling were partially crushed by the tree. The debris landed on desk surfaces, but with the exception of one computer monitor, none of the workstations were damaged.

Chapter 6: Securing Wireless Networks

Wireless networking has experienced huge growth in recent years. Anyone with a basic network connection—whether through dial-up, ADSL, DSL, cable, or satellite—can inexpensively network desktops and laptops at home or in a small office environment. Most laptops have built-in wireless networking interface cards and, for about $20, a wireless networking interface card can be installed in either a desktop or laptop.

Wireless networking depends on equipment that is slightly different from standard hardwired networking. The Internet connection enters at the same demarcation point and is distributed through a cable modem, and then usually to a router. The router distributes the IP addresses to the computers on the network. The wireless access point device then distributes the data over the network via radio waves.

Radio waves are nothing more than the distribution of low-voltage electricity from a transmitter to a receiver. It's the same principle as the little AM radio I once used to listen to the Seattle Pilots baseball team in the woodshed. (That is, before they left Seattle to become the Milwaukee Brewers. Yes, I have let go and forgiven them.)

The range of these radio waves depends on what is known as the hertz range, or the frequency of the radio waves. Wi-Fi is now distributed at 2.4 gigahertz and has an effective "clear-shot" range of 300 feet. The effective distribution range diminishes for every wall, ceiling, or roof the frequency must travel through. Generally, each solid obstruction reduces the effective range by about 50–100 feet.

Whenever I need immediate Internet access but am not at home or work, I boot my laptop and search for wireless networks within an effective range. I look for public wireless networks that are configured to allow anyone with a proper network interface card to connect to the network and access the Internet.

Some businesses and schools set up wireless access for customers and students. An administrator must create an access account for the users, which can be either free or for a fee. These networks are slightly more secure than public wireless networks because they require access to password-protected accounts.

It is easy to understand how a wireless network's security is an issue. Even if a wireless network may not be a specific target for hacking, this is simply not enough assurance. Data transmitted and stored on a wireless network is extremely vulnerable. Unsecured wireless networks use the public airwaves at 2.4 gigahertz, and many laptops and handheld devices can receive and transmit over this network. No law exists to prohibit connecting to a wireless network that has not been secured. However, it is against the law to gain illicit access to any computer or other kind of node on a wireless network, which creates a security dilemma.

As described in chapter 1, there are very inexpensive chat-sniffing applications that allow anyone to capture and read in real time most chat messages that are sent over a wireless network. A computer does not necessarily need to be connected to the network to capture the messages. However, allowing unsecured access to a wireless network publicizes the IP addressing configuration for the network, thereby making the chat-sniffing even easier. If the chat messages are not encrypted and are transmitted over a wireless network, they are in the public domain. If a person subsequently uses the information for some illicit or illegal activity, then he or she has broken the law.

One method commonly used to secure access to a wireless network is encrypting an access control password using wired equivalency protection (WEP) or Wi-Fi-protected access (WPA). If you do not have the specific key to enable your computer to send and receive encrypted data for a given network, you do not have permission to use that network. Using WEP and WPA is explained later in this chapter, but it is important to understand how these encryption methods are touted.

Some security specialists claim that once WEP or WPA is enabled, all data crossing over the network is then encrypted; this is not the case at all. Other applications must be used to encrypt specific data. WEP and WPA merely encrypt access permissions and restrict access to the network. It is also well known among hackers that WEP can be "cracked" in a matter of minutes, giving the hacker easy access to network services. Obviously, it is illegal to access a computer network that has been specifically restricted to certain users.

Again, there is no guarantee that, once practices for securing a wireless network have been put into place, someone will not gain access to your network.

Nevertheless, it does provide you with some safeguards. Begin to secure the wireless network with the following:

- Enable WEP or WPA
- Disable DHCP on the wireless system
- Stop the broadcasting of the SSID for the wireless network
- Use MAC-address filtering
- Use complex administrative passwords
- Reduce the effective range of distribution

ENABLING WEP OR WPA

Most wireless access points now require some configuration. These are the usual steps:

1. During configuration, among other things, the user is asked to implement WEP or WPA. Put simply, WPA is a more rigorous encryption and should be used. It will slow down virtually all but a few hackers, who would have to be desperate to sit and run a password-cracking application for an hour or more trying to gain access.

2. The installation software generates an encryption key. Write this down; it is the key that must be entered into the wireless administration application in the computer. This application comes with the wireless network interface card and is used to manage all wireless network connections.

3. To gain access to the wireless network after WPA has been installed, a dialog box will

appear as the user attempts to access the network. This is where the trusted user enters the encryption key. In a commercial environment, it would be wise to give this key only to the administrator and allow him or her to enter the key as each new user must gain access.

4. Once the key has been entered, the user is considered trusted and will be allowed access to the network until the key is changed. In chapter 28 on policies, I will cover briefly the need to regularly change encrypted access control keys, especially if a disgruntled employee leaves.

DISABLING DHCP ON THE WIRELESS SYSTEM

A protocol is used to hand out IP addresses to computers on a network. It exists in the router, and could also exist in a switch or a server. Once a computer is configured and authenticated, the IP address is given to the network interface card and the computer can access networking services.

There is a difference between a public IP address and a private IP address sequence. Public IP addresses can be seen by other computers on different networks. Private addresses are not seen externally and cannot really access the Internet unless they are routed through one public address. Most wireless devices that distribute IP addresses use one external public address and give all connected computers a private address. These private addresses are within a specific numeric range. If a computer can see data transmitting over a wireless network, it can detect the addressing. In this way, a hacker can sniff a specific range of computers using these addresses, and this makes it easier to capture chat messages, email, and other types of data.

If the administrator turns off the DHCP for IP addressing, then a static address will need to be entered in the network interface card. This static address will be configured in the router to allow the trusted computer to access networking services. Static addresses do not need to follow any pattern. This practice does not allow a chat-sniffing application or other type of detection application to determine an IP address on the network.

STOPPING THE BROADCASTING OF THE SSID FOR THE WIRELESS NETWORK

Most configurable wireless access points or routers allow for the choice to broadcast or not broadcast the SSID, or service set identifier. If someone searches for wireless networks and you are broadcasting the name of yours, it will appear in the list of available networks they can see. If you choose not to broadcast, the person will not see your wireless system and will not attempt to connect.

However, it is very important for the administrator to remember what the SSID for the system is. It is also advisable to change the default SSID to some complex name and then to retain that name in a secure environment along with the WPA. When a new user is connected to the wireless network, the administrator will need to enter both the SSID and the encrypted key. Again, this SSID can be changed at will, but then the new name will need to be entered into all computers in order to gain access.

ENABLING MAC-ADDRESS FILTERING

To gain access to a network, a computer needs a network interface card with a unique MAC address. A MAC address is a unique value associated with a network adapter; it uniquely identifies an adapter on the local network. The MAC address is often listed as the machine address of the computer. This address is complex enough so that no two computers will have the same one. However, removing and installing the network interface card in another computer will assign the MAC address to that computer.

Even if someone outside your network can see your wireless network, if your MAC addresses are not listed, that person cannot access any services or information on the wireless network. Nonetheless, some of the more complex configurable wireless access points or wireless routers provide the opportunity to list the trusted MAC addresses. The administrator can find the MAC address quite easily on each computer in order to enter it into the list. In a Windows environment, for instance, the administrator runs the Command prompt, enters ipconfig /all, and the computer lists the IP and MAC address for the associated computer. In the same way, to block a computer from accessing the network, the administrator can simply remove the MAC address from the list.

USING COMPLEX ADMINISTRATIVE
PASSWORDS

As a test, students of computer science are often told to test the administrative password patterns of a given system. They are told to enter 'Administrator' in the user name

59

field, and then to enter two different passwords. The first is 'Password,' but if they have not gained access to the system, they must enter 'God.' In recent years, these two passwords would have granted access to almost 8 percent of all managed networks. Fortunately, the word is out; create complex alpha-numeric passwords and memorize them.

Password-cracking software applications are easily obtained, and the more complex the password, the more difficult they are to crack. A good practice is to create a password that is at least 16 characters long and contains lowercase letters, capitalized letters, numbers, and keyboard symbols. It is also wise to maintain these passwords in the same secure environment as the WPA and SSID.

REDUCING THE EFFECTIVE RANGE OF DISTRIBUTION

Most wireless access points and routers will allow the owner to reduce the output, thereby effectively reducing the range. Limiting the range of your wireless network can be advantageous because it will also limit the number of people who can see your network. Knowing that every wall, floor, ceiling, or roof will reduce the effective range, position the wireless access points where legitimate users will gain access but outsiders will not even see a signal. A good test of this is to take a wireless device outside the premises and continuously adjust the location or output until it cannot be detected by anyone but authorized users.

CONCLUSION

While these practices do not necessarily guarantee the security of a wireless network, when used together, they help to increase the probability that potential illicit users will neither see the network nor gain access to it.

Chapter 7: Protecting a Network from Viruses and Malware

For many years, conventional wisdom warned strictly against viruses attached to emails. There was relatively little emphasis placed on more pernicious attacks on personal and company-owned data and assets. When I taught programming, I wanted my students to understand that a program can be written to do just about anything. For instance, I offered one class an extra-credit project: Write a program that searches for personal data in a standard Windows directory structure. Many succeeded in doing so.

In a more advanced programming class, these same students were offered another extra-credit project: Write a program that can piggyback an email attachment undetected and locate itself in a file or directory, from where it can monitor and log users' Internet activity. The program also was occasionally to send a log file to a specific port on another computer. Three students were amazingly successful. While this program might be perceived as intrusive, there are legitimate applications for it. For instance, a parent might want to be able to monitor the Internet activity on all home computers. As a network administrator, I have used similar log files regularly to monitor employee Internet access.

In the wrong hands, this type of malware—known as a *spybot*— functions as a monitor for illicit purposes. It is not necessarily programmed to destroy data or diminish hardware functionality; its primary function is to collect specific types of data. The viruses of the late 1990s were brute-force attacks on data and infrastructure. Downloading patches and antivirus updates once did a fairly good job of protecting our computers from this type of malicious attack. However, with the rise of identity theft, corporate spying, and data mining, the plan of attack has changed dramatically. Instead of destroying the data, it has become more valuable to steal the data over long periods of time.

Many virtual communities and information-based sites want to personalize your user experience, so they ask you to create a membership profile. To reduce the number of passwords you need to memorize, these sites offer to place a cookie on your computer that holds your user name and password. Early on, cookies were seen as necessary to speed up the return to any given website, especially a site where a user indicates that his or her user name and password should be remembered. When the user launches the site, a program running on the site searches for the cookie and reads the user name and password. The program then places them in the proper dialogue box. Within a few seconds, the user is logged in.

Imagine the power of such a program in the wrong hands. A well-skilled programmer can use this same framework to write a program that the user does not voluntarily download. The program reads every keystroke on the user's computer and logs them in plain text. They don't stop there. The program might identify banking, tax, legal and investment accounts, and copy this material to a log that is accessible to someone at a website that the user visits regularly.

Behind the scenes, banks, schools, and government agencies are dealing with this issue. The primary source of this type of attack is not necessarily external; in fact, the majority of these come from inside the network. For instance, one financial aid administrator for a private school hired an individual who had extensive experience with federal financial-aid programs. The employee was secretly on the payroll of a competing school. During his tenure, the employee placed five or more spybots on other financial-aid workstations. The competing school was then able to track certain types of data transactions, which informed them of real numbers for enrollment, the percentage of self-pay versus financial-aid students, and other useful data. Fortunately, the network administrator conducted regular audits of installed applications and discovered the programs.

Many users have become aware of these issues, but have not completely educated themselves on how to protect their networking environments. The beginning is easy: Get industry-tested antivirus software for the network and individual workstations, and then schedule the updates for these applications as they become available from the manufacturer. The next step is to find and install security applications that specifically focus on spybots, cookies, malware, and other types of data-mining applications that fall outside the category of a virus.

I have used Spybot Search and Destroy (Spybot-S&D), which effectively and regularly scans my hard drive for these types of applications. Research various web browsers. Use Mozilla Firefox as your web browser, along with its companion, Stopzilla, which can be configured to monitor cookies, spybots, and other types of malware in real time. These products have proven to be fairly successful in keeping abreast of new versions of these problematic applications. If you use Microsoft's Internet Explorer as your default browser, go to the Microsoft website and search for information and downloads for securing IE. This browser has known vulnerabilities, but Microsoft works diligently to patch them.

If you are managing a networked environment and choose to pay for automatic updating of antivirus protection and applications that clean spybots and cookies, prepare other users' computers in advance to make sure they are able to receive the updates properly. The upcoming chapter on policies will review how to work effectively with companies of 1,000–5,000 employees to succeed in thoroughly updating this protection.

Chapter 8: Understanding Hacking and Cracking

True hackers want their good reputations back; people who should be termed *crackers* have hijacked it. The crackers are the folks who break into or simply break computer systems and destroy data. Hackers have long prided themselves on being creators and problem-solvers. The true hacking community does not advocate breaking into, stealing, disrupting, or in any way illicitly or illegally gaining access to systems. They advocate real problem-solving to make computing easier and more effective.

Crackers, on the other hand, want exactly the opposite. They advocate grossly illegal activity directed at computer systems. They call themselves hackers, but they are not that good at what they do; they do not deserve the title. A cracker with a high level of programming and networking skills can do damage, undoubtedly. Individuals with the highest skill sets in the IT world are responsible for the well-publicized and secret case studies of data destruction, data theft, infrastructure damage, and planted viruses.

A system is vulnerable to these kinds of focused attacks if specific conditions are present. First, open ports are an invitation to crackers—a widely broadcasted invitation. Crackers routinely scan ports and then access the target computer quite easily if those ports are open. The protocol that is the underlying engine for instant messaging, H.323, runs in what is known as *promiscuous mode*. The port it uses to communicate with other computers is always open and receptive, especially if the chat is idle. The protocol is designed to allow almost any kind of file to pass into the computer through the open port. Users at the application level see that they need to give permission to download pictures or documents through instant messaging, but in reality, the protocol allows any file to enter through that port.

Second, crackers search for administrative access that has not been locked down, such as an administrative account left logged in or a simple, easy-to-guess password. If a cracker can access a server, he or she can easily get into it, as long as the administrator is not constantly monitoring for intrusions. Once a cracker has administrative access to any server on a system, he or she has access to everything. One simple principle to understand is that permissions migrate; that is, an administrator on one server could very well be the administrator on any other system connected to that server.

Next, crackers are great social engineers, and they need your passwords. They need you to feel as though you could trust them with your children, let alone your password. The crackers I have caught are intelligent, good-looking, affable, party-going males and females (as opposed to the stereotype of crackers being socially inept teens living in their parents' basements), who gain your confidence and then attack. Allowing them privileged access to an area with one or more workstations—or a server room—is the beginning of the end. When I meet a very bright and charming information technologist who is all too willing to do favors for me, I am immediately—yet privately—cautious. This innate suspicion has served me in identifying and isolating two crackers before they could attack.

Lastly, crackers are adept at getting work where they need to steal or wreak havoc. One situation I am aware of involved a smooth, handsome, and technically very bright young man. The owner of the financial advising company felt assured by hiring him as an IT executive. The new executive had nefarious intentions from the start. He knew the value of the client list, and then succeeded in befriending a disgruntled vice president. Together, they gained access to the entire client database and copied it. The FBI has been brought in to investigate the situation.

Let's dispel some more myths about hacking and cracking. If your home computer contains valuable unsecured data, you could well be cracked. If your company has any data that might be of value to someone, you will witness an attempt—successful or not—to crack that system. If your company takes effective and easily applied measures to harden the external perimeter, the cracker will probably not succeed unless he or she is inside your company's network.

We will discuss perimeter and zone security in more detail later in this book. For now, for home or small-business networks, we will describe two important but easily managed tasks.

First, if you can manage your router, block all but the most essential ports. Port 80 is your Internet access and, if that is all you use the router for, then block everything else. If you need to use instant messaging, find out which port it runs on and leave it open; however, remember to manage your instant messaging by encrypting messages and turning the application off when a chat is finished. If you do not have a manageable router and are using a Windows operating system, go to the Microsoft website and research methods for closing ports for your operating system.

Next, check with the manufacturer of your operating system to see if there is a resident firewall. If there is, research how to configure the resident firewall in the operating system to allow acceptable activity and disallow external access. Do the research before you start switching the settings of your firewall. If the firewall disallows VPN, Internet access, and file sharing after you've reconfigured it then you did not reconfigure the firewall correctly.

Once you have closed ports and used a resident firewall application, your system is secure from most crackers. Now you need to deal with your bigger problem: in-house accidental crackers. Some people within the network, simply out of boredom, click through to unfamiliar drives to see what they can access. They fiddle around a bit and then accidentally change the content of a folder. If an administrator has not set proper permissions, these accidental crackers can gain access to financial data and compromise the privacy of the company.

Far more sinister is the help desk person who understands directory structures and finds a backdoor to sensitive information. With a bit of social engineering—finding someone's user name and password information within arm's reach of a workstation, for example—the perpetrator logs in after volunteering to work the lonely late shift. The deed is done and the cracker remains undetected.

Any network administrator who believes that the biggest problem involving crackers is outside the network's perimeter is inviting disaster.

SECTION II
ADVANCED ISSUES IN
NETWORK SECURITY

Chapter 9: Implementing Access Control Mechanisms

The concept of access control is relatively easy to understand unless you get your information from the vendors of hardware and software solutions. You will be in a better position to analyze your access-control mechanisms and policies if you begin with the theory and then approach vendors from that perspective.

There are two general types of vulnerabilities regarding access to a network: unauthorized users and unauthorized nodes or elements.

UNAUTHORIZED USERS

In any business environment, employees and certain categories of contractors are given permission to use the business's computing resources. This permission should be commensurate with the level of authority and responsibility that each person has in the company. A hierarchy of permissions will determine what level of access any given individual should have.

Remote (off-site) access to a computer network offers some unique challenges. While the user may have certain access rights and permissions, the method of transferring the data or accessing the network remotely may inadvertently grant access to the wrong individual. If a virtual private network is improperly configured or if administrators do not clearly think through the issue of inheritance of permissions, then access issues can arise.

Permissions migrate across a network backbone. If a person is granted administrative privileges on one server, then other servers on the same backbone could see this person as an administrator. There are several lockdown solutions that administrators can apply to slow down computing services and take away privileges.

Guest accounts on systems have proven to be problematic for network administrators; I strongly advocate against the use of them. A guest account is an invitation to bypass policies and perform illicit activities under an anonymous user name. A guest may be a very capable cracker who has the ability to challenge authentication systems and crack an administrative password. Because guests are anonymous, as long as the network has unrestricted access to the Internet, they can explore and download whatever they like without anyone knowing. The responsibility of those downloads falls both on the administrator and the owner of the computing system. Unless the administrator has irrefutable evidence that one individual was using a specific workstation when the illicit activity occurred, there is no way to prove the source of this activity.

One common method of mitigating illegal access to files, folders, drives, or servers is to deploy log-management devices or software. This type of software allows you to monitor any portion of your PC, small network, or large-scale enterprise network. Splunk is easy to set up, deploy, and monitor; you can download it for free at *www.splunk.com*, and the pricing increases based on the number of users and the amount of data collected. Splunk can be solely focused on those attempting to access the network you are monitoring. Splunk's supporting documentation suggests that all users should have a unique account and user name so that auditing the files for illicit access will be easier.

UNAUTHORIZED NODES OR ELEMENTS

Three competing electronic device manufacturers have each developed unique network analyzers. These analyzers are equipped with powerful software applications that are intended to give legitimate users valuable information about every node on a wide area network. Once plugged into an RJ45 wall jack, the user can see and analyze every node on the system without authentication. The data received back to the device can include: IP addresses and subnets; names of computers or other nodes; operating systems running; file structures used on each node; MAC addresses; user names; and even passwords if they are not hidden. These devices and applications are intended for legitimate security analyses and to map out potential bottlenecks in a network. Even though they are costly to acquire, imagine how these devices can be abused.

A privately owned laptop could easily be masked to appear as if it is a company-owned asset. The laptop could be equipped with password-cracking software for operating systems or wireless networks, or it could simply be on the network utilizing resources illicitly. If the device is granted an IP address, the user may not be able to authenticate to the system, but the node can monitor data traffic on the system, such as when chat-sniffing on a wireless network.

Authenticating nodes or elements on a network is equally as important as authenticating users, but can be more difficult. Let's address the users first.

ACCESS CONTROL MECHANISMS

Anyone using a network should have a user name that is associated with a secure database with a private, complex password. The two elements—database and password—are the very foundation of an effective access control policy, as well as the most violated.

User name conventions are not an issue; someone can try to pretend to be a user by assuming the naming convention, but if the name does not exist in the database, then they cannot acquire access. The real issue is in the security of the database. If the database is searchable, it will likely be compromised. For instance, in UNIX/Linux, the default location for the database is /bin, so any good administrator will change the location and the path immediately. In Windows, there are various methods for the owner of the computer to hide his or her password. (The Microsoft website gives detailed technical information about hiding password files so that they are still available for authentication.) While this is an essential step in providing secure access control, it is not the most troublesome.

Password management is an issue for every network administrator. A password should have at least three of four possible elements:

1. Capital letters
2. Lowercase letters

3. Numbers
4. Keyboard characters, with some exceptions

The password should be at least 12 characters long and the sequence of the characters should be as random as possible while still making it simple for the user to memorize it. Do the math; password-cracking software is based on math algorithms that query each character of the password with these questions:

- Are you a lowercase letter a–z?
- Are you a capital letter A–Z?
- Are you a number 1–9?
- Are you a keyboard character?

The cracking software then looks for patterns, something similar to the game show *Wheel of Fortune*. If the pattern appears quickly, the software begins to guess and—bingo!—the person is in. A fast computer can go through the password-cracking process fairly quickly, so the more characters you use and the more random the sequence, the more difficult it is to guess the password.

However, this assumes that someone needs to use password-cracking software. The worst abuse of passwords is sheer laziness, particularly if people write the password down and place it under a keyboard or in a nearby drawer. Some of the most notorious system cracks occurred when someone was planted as a member of an office cleaning crew and given specific instructions to find passwords. Good password management requires memorization or very secure lockup.

An alternative to passwords is biometrics, or the use of eye scanners and fingerprints to identify people. Many people object to the use of these devices and, while they are very accurate in authenticating individuals, I know of at least three employers who have either dismantled their biometric authentication or chose to stay with a password-based authentication system because of these concerns. Others have experimented with pass-cards, which pose a problem because they can be stolen, or combining pass-cards with traditional passwords to add a layer of security to the authentication process.

Rogue elements or unauthorized nodes are more serious threats to security than compromised passwords. A network should be able to:

- detect new elements;
- determine if the elements should be allowed access;
- allow or deny access based on clearly defined policies;
- quarantine rogue elements;
- locate exactly where the elements are; and
- read the MAC addresses that are requesting IP addresses.

Most server software comes with tools that will recognize rogue elements and unauthorized nodes. There are numerous methods and third-party products available for accomplishing this type of routine. If you do not have a system in place to handle these tasks, find a method or vendor to implement one. Network inventory applications such as Alchemy Network Inventory and Total Network

Monitor are usable for small-scale networks and can be expanded to work for larger enterprise networks as well.

Access control is more than logging in to a system. Access control systems should control any type of access to your network. After completing the system assessment, an administrator should be able to pull information from various areas of the assessment and determine if there are adequate access controls. The assessment will point out two areas of concern: the perimeter and any internal zones of the network. Chapter 10 looks at these areas.

Chapter 10: Implementing Perimeter and Zone Security

Think of a computer network as a baseball stadium. If I wanted to boo the Boston Red Sox from San Diego's PETCO Field, I would buy a ticket in the cheap seats. There are a couple good restaurants I like there, so before I give my ticket to the taker, I buy something to go. The sidewalk around the perimeter of PETCO Field reveals that there is a grassy area where people can watch the game live for free, even though the view isn't great.

I usually buy tickets for the third tier above first base. My ticket is a specific color with a specific section and seat number on it. I give my ticket to the taker, who examines my take-out food bag for weapons and booze, and I am in. I walk around the internal walkways until I find the correct section and my specific seat. Once the Red Sox are on the field, I can boo to my heart's delight.

This scenario describes a pretty good perimeter and zone architecture. If I try to jump through the ticket booths, there are enough security guards on hand to tackle me and throw me out. I doubt very many people have succeeded in "climbing the fence" of a modern ballpark; the perimeter is fairly secure. Add to that any rogue elements I might be carrying in my bag. While the security check is not optimum, it is effective.

Until the owner of the first-tier tickets kicks me out, I might be able to sneak into his box seats. The usher would probably tell me to go upstairs where my section is. If I kept trying to sit in a better section but did not have the proper ticket, I would eventually be thrown out of the park. This is a good example of the theory of zone security.

The perimeter of a network is the first point of entry at the demarcation point and the first screening hardware found in the server room. This equipment could be a simple router with access control lists or a firebox, a piece of networking hardware with vendor-specific firmware that serves as a gateway for authenticating users outside the system and blocking specific kinds of activity. A firewall, a piece of software installed in the router or server, could also create a perimeter.

In any given organization, there can be multiple perimeters. For business reasons, separate access lines can be installed for specific activities. In a university, I might bring in one or more access lines to the demarcation point for student access to the Internet. One may be specifically designated for wireless activity, one or more lines may be for academic access, and then one or more may serve the business needs of the university. Each of these access lines could be treated separately with their own firebox, firewall, access-controlled router or switch, effectively and completely separating business functions, *i.e.,* the students would never see the networks serving the academic or business sides.

This kind of architecture has loosely been referred to as a DMZ, or demilitarized zone. This term comes from military jargon and refers to an area where no one is allowed unless both sides of the conflict agree there is a need. The concept is applied to networks in various ways. Administrators separate various servers or segments of a network from the typical user and refer to it as a DMZ. In our university scenario, the business servers containing all the financial and compliance data of the school would probably be behind a DMZ where only a few top-level administrators would have access.

There is no exact right way to design a secure perimeter. A perimeter can be as secure as an organization desires and/or can afford. Perimeter security is good for keeping external problems out of the system; however, this might solve only 15 percent of the problem at best.

There can be any combination of routers, switches, bridges, and hubs that divide the network into specific zones. Server operating systems such as UNIX, Linux, or Windows can be configured into zones based on levels of access needed and subnets. Dividing an internal system into zones has been effective in segregating most users into their appropriate areas of concern and responsibility, particularly for those employees and users who diligently work without straying into areas that do not relate to them. If users cannot see a server containing sensitive data in their internal browser, then they probably will not attempt to access it. A zone can be easily configured to hide segments of the network. If users can see the server and they know accessing it is not allowed, most do not try.

So far, zone security has kept honest people at bay. Perimeter security has effectively kept out external malicious attacks, viruses, spybots, and other undesirables. What have not been effectively addressed yet are the unauthorized user and the rogue element. I recommend that administrators rethink the concept of a pure external perimeter and precise internal zones. Taking on the problems of unauthorized internal access and rogue elements requires us to see the inside as having multiple perimeters and the outside as potentially being divided into several zones.

Consider those who provide security for elected officials. If I want to meet the President of the United States, I must pass through multiple zones, crossing security perimeters at each zone and maybe even multiple perimeters at each edge of a zone until I finally stand in the Oval Office and shake his hand. A secure computing environment might be configured so that there are different authenticating servers for each zone that a user wants to enter. There might be internal firewalls or fireboxes at every zone edge. Good password policy for this type of environment would include requiring a separate password for every authenticating server, and perhaps even a different naming convention for every perimeter checkpoint. Inside the routers, there could then still be access control lists that are specific to the user and MAC address. There could also be an application keeping constant vigil over the entire network, looking for elements not previously authenticated to the system, and isolating them. If the elements cannot be validated, they might be permanently blocked from accessing certain zones.

The configuration described in the previous paragraph might be the foundation of a system holding research and development data for special weapons. As tight as it may seem to be, it might still require more layers of security. Effective security of perimeters and zones requires careful thought. I could give you a recipe here for specific configurations, but it may not serve your purposes. Perhaps you have a web server hosting a wiki community where users enter data and alter the site at will. Extremely tight perimeter and zone security might not be the effective answer.

The more connections a system has both internally and externally the more at risk it is. A computer with no Internet access and not networked to any other computer, standing alone inside a locked closet inside the locked office of the owner, is a fairly secure system. It might not be a practical system for most business needs, but it is secure behind a physical perimeter and within a locked, fireproof zone.

All of this is moot in an atmosphere of slack management. I have seen complex perimeter and zone security configured for an airtight network only to find the server room door unlocked (and, in one case, no door on the server room at all) and passwords scribbled on the wall. If this is your idea of a "casual working environment," don't bother with security.

As we move into the next topic, it will become apparent that more complex security of computer networks requires fully integrated thinking. As we discuss extranets, intranets, and web portals, consider these in light of access control and perimeter/zone security.

Chapter 11: Designing Secure Intranets, Extranets, and Web Portals

Extranets and intranets are used to disseminate information directly to employees through company-controlled websites not accessible to persons outside the company. Virtual private networks (VPNs) use a public telecommunication infrastructure such as the Internet to provide remote offices or individual users with secure access to their organization's network. The VPN is an address-based direct connection between a remote computer and specific hardware assets on the network.

Using this technology, a network administrator can easily access certain servers and remotely manage or monitor activity, and someone in the finance department can access specific folders and generate reports while on a business trip. Remote access has become a staple of every business.

Accessing these servers, whether inside the main office where the servers reside or from a remote location—either company-owned or otherwise—presents some unique security challenges. Websites governed by the company for internal use might contain data that is considered a trade secret, sensitive to national security, or of a personal nature. For instance, it is relatively easy to share drawings for a fighter jet with qualified viewers. Distributed applications, especially in design and drafting, allow multiple users to view and manipulate drawings at the same time. While this might be an extremely efficient way of doing business, the risk lies in giving access to the wrong person.

Early experiments in video chat rooms that allowed up to 16 users to see and hear each other proved that consistent bandwidth was the key to ensuring that the experience was the same for all participants. Users with very low dial-up bandwidth complained that the data was coming too slow and that they missed a lot of the video or the audio portions. People with fiber-optic connections complained that there was often a two- or three-minute delay from a user with slow bandwidth.

The technology underlying an extranet that allows multiple users to access data simultaneously finds it roots in those early-Internet broadcasting experiences. The IP and MAC addresses of authenticated users are queued and each connection receives the data simultaneously by blending within the server. It was easier to implement this type of extranet technology in a tightly controlled corporate environment where the bandwidth to all locations was consistent. Once the data flows out of the corporate web server to the participants, their individual locations become perimeters. The extranet has virtually extended the perimeter of the network as far as the most remote participant.

For example, designers involved in the development of the Boeing 7E7 project resided in several different parts of the world and could, at a designated time, meet virtually to discuss extremely sensitive details about the jet. The protocols for much of this technology are of concern. Much like chat, if any one of the participants was using a wireless connection that was not fully encrypted, someone could easily intercept the text or graphics portions of the session.

A *stateful connection* is one in which some information about a connection between two systems is retained for future use; in some cases, the connection might be kept open even if the two systems are not transmitting data. A stateful connection is essentially the same as a connection that is used for chat sessions but it uses a different protocol. At face value, the VPN connection is nothing more than a stateful session between two designated ports. The VPN configuration software is embedded in an operating system such as Windows, which establishes a direct, stateful connection between two computers once an IP and MAC address are entered. If the data passed through the VPN is not hidden in some way, anyone who can sniff this connection can read the data. VPNs are fairly secure when dealing with honest people, but they are not secure when the connection is subject to port scans, vampire taps, session hijacking, if the VPN session is improperly configured, or if unauthorized users are connected.

Technological advances often outpace security. As carefully as a plan to secure a new technology is made, someone will attempt to circumvent the security to illicitly access data and assets. New technologies demand rethinking access-control methods because they extend the perimeter of the network to unplanned distances.

A response to this is relatively simple: Encrypt the data. In order words, plan to modify the data somehow at one end using a secret key, and share the key with only trusted computers or individuals, who will then decrypt the data at the other end. A good mathematician will need to create the encryption methods and secret keys.

One method for securing VPNs is based on a simple concept: multiprotocol label switching (MPLS). Using switches rather than routers, labels are placed on the data packets that encrypt them. Switches quickly send data directly to a specific MAC address rather than through access control lists in a router and then through a polling process in a hub. The packets are then sent to specific MAC addresses entered into the configuration. The recipient has the private key and decrypts the data.

Encrypted data transmitted by an extranet or across a VPN is handled nicely by third-party products or through various new technologies. Cisco, Linksys, Netgear, and DLink have done a great job of building affordable and configurable switches that will allow deployment of MPLS on a small- to medium-sized network. The small switches used at home or in a small business will adequately service 2 to 100 users in one location. For larger enterprise-class networks, Cisco is a fantastic solution for faster, more accurate MPLS.

While this type of security—which is replicated in various ways by other hardware and software manufacturers—is effective at face value, never lose sight of the problems of illicit access to a system, social engineering, and careless configuration. Some perpetrators are extremely patient and wait for an opportunity to arise, immediately capitalizing on it.

Chapter 12: Implementing System Monitoring

System monitoring is as important as flossing your teeth. Nevertheless, how many administrators do you think floss their teeth every day? This chapter divides the subject of monitoring into three distinct types of monitoring, each equally important:

- Monitoring for performance
- Proactive monitoring of external attacks at the perimeter
- Actively monitoring users inside the system

Each type of monitoring uses different tools and the results of the monitoring are each interpreted differently. Performance is typically a mechanical issue, a question of whether or not all the essential distribution nodes are plugged in, turned on, and functional as well as if all the cables are passing data. External threats are monitored at the point of entry using routers, switches, fireboxes, and firewalls. Sadly, application tools do not readily support internal monitoring of users because the demand for such tools has been for performance and external-threat monitoring.

I once learned of an incident where a sensitive server was compromised; client data was copied and stolen. The loss was multifaceted. The actual loss of the data caused an interruption in regular business activity. It was costly to restore the data, much of which was not backed up. Major clients lost trust in the firm, and the investigation was expensive. I do not know all the details of the case—

nor should I; however, it is clear that someone inside the system perpetrated the incident. The access control was not properly configured and a user accessed the data files.

There was no key logging or other type of monitoring system in place. The only monitoring system being used was for performance and passive monitoring of intrusions at the perimeter. There was no internal monitoring of user activity, nor did the company log access attempts at any of the data files. The administrators of that system determined that they needed another level of security.

Whenever the issue of user monitoring is raised, many people focus on illicit or illegal Internet activity. In fact, user monitoring should focus on the files, folders, directories, drives, and servers users can or attempt to access. Once decisions are made about each user's level of access, the configuration of permissions requires careful attention.

Budgetary constraints are often cited as the primary reason for not proactively monitoring user activity. In many cases, however, time and resources are deployed instead to monitor external attacks against systems that have already been hardened. (*Harden a system* means eliminating as many security risks as possible from it, by removing nonessential software and utilities, disabling guest accounts, implementing secure passwords, and so on.)

Internal monitoring is not popular. Tracking what employees do throughout the day after logging into the system always raises privacy issues. People do not like the concept of "Big Brother" watching. Even if there is full disclosure of monitoring during the hiring process, employees may still complain. Managers have to balance this anxiety with the likelihood that roughly 85 percent of security problems come from inside the system.

Be assured that internal monitoring is as crucial as external. A junior administrator I once worked with spent his time monitoring external pings and port scans launched against his system, while ignoring internal security. He proudly claimed that no external activity could penetrate the system and that the perimeter was locked down fairly tightly. I then pointed out that, during my system assessment, I discovered everyone within the system had access to a folder containing information about the company's pending initial public offering. The data had been copied, but there was no log of users who had gained access to the folder, which was potentially a serious violation of the Security and Exchange Commission's laws governing the public offering of company stock. In my security analysis report, I identified that the external perimeter was relatively secure, but that there was no internal security for the most sensitive data.

Here is a checklist of basic items and activity that should be monitored on a regular basis:

- **PERFORMANCE**
  - *System Through-Put*
  Find the total capacity of data through-put of the system and whether there are any breaks or bottlenecks.
  - *Quality of Service (QoS)*
  When there is scheduled demand for bandwidth dedication for the transfer of sensitive or large amounts of data, monitor

the system prior to and during the scheduled transfer to ensure adequate QoS.

o *Node Capacity*

Monitor the processes on mission-critical nodes (router, switch, bridge, firebox, and server) to ensure adequate system hardware for critical demands.

- **EXTERNAL MONITORING**
    o *Port Scans*

    Monitor all attempted port scans and gather source data of the scanner.

    o *Viruses, Bots, Rootkits, and Trojans*

    Monitor all incoming data, including data transfers, attachments, email messages, and chat sessions at the point of entry for any malicious code.

    o *Remote Access*

    Monitor all remote access attempts. Log all attempts whether successful or not. Monitor and log all valid and illicit user names, passwords, crack attempts, and all successful and unsuccessful password attempts.

    o *Remote Access Activity*

    Monitor and log all remote access activity, including all file, folder, directory, and drive access.

- **INTERNAL MONITORING**
    o *Data Access*

Monitor and log all access attempts to sensitive data, which can be used later to determine legitimate or illicit access.

o *Logins*

Monitor and log all logins. Employees are fairly habitual about times when they start and stop work. Anomalous activity may point to identity spoofing or illicit login attempts.

o *Internal Virus Infections*

Monitor all internal traffic for the introduction of viruses, bots, rootkits, and Trojans from user-owned and transferred storage devices.

o *Internet Activity*

If there is a policy in place, monitor Internet traffic for compliance.

Current Windows server software has a built-in tool for monitoring. I started using the *PerfMon* tool in Windows 2000 and it has since developed into a more broad-reaching tool. System monitor and performance monitor are two other built-in monitors within Windows.

There are several third-party applications that will easily handle any one of these monitoring activities. When shopping monitoring products, compare like features and determine how much monitoring you will effectively need. (By *effectively*, I mean too much tool provides too much data in a small network; often people will stop using the tool because it is too much work. Scale your monitoring tools to your specific needs.)

- Orion Network Performance Monitor by Solarwinds is a comprehensive monitoring tool that is easy to setup and use. Their pricing structure allows for small deployments at a very reasonable cost, which can then build up to larger multi-location deployments.
- Overseer Network Monitor is more specifically designed for smaller installations. It is very affordable for homes or small businesses. Overseer does not have a fancy dashboard, but the eye-catching graphics give a feature-rich, understandable interface.

Chapter 13: Implementing Backup, Storage, and Recovery Procedures

My mother used to say that it was a good thing I didn't have a twin because two of me would be too much. I can't say the same thing about data. Having two or three exact copies of every important piece of data is essential.

While I was completing my master's degree, I worked for a virtual library managing their Linux download center. Fellow classmates knew that I was handy with a computer, so when they would lose or corrupt an important paper the night before it was due, they called on me. They wanted me to perform magic and get the paper back to its original condition. Unfortunately, if they hadn't backed up their drafts, these students quickly learned the importance of doing so in the future.

A few astute financial investment firms located in the World Trade Center in New York City were operational just a week after the incident, partly due to the topics covered later in this book and to regular, safe backup and storage of all data. I was particularly happy with one company; they managed my meager investments!

BACKUPS

There is no excuse for not having a copy of important data and regular backups are essential. There are three principle types of backups:

1. Incremental
2. Differential
3. Full

The differences between incremental and differential are subtle. Incremental catches all data added or changed after the last incremental backup; this type is done frequently. Differential catches all changes to existing data after a full backup. The full backup, of course, is just as it sounds: A complete backup of the entire system. Some administrators do not implement differential backups and are satisfied with incremental and full. A good practice is to back up the system using what is called a *day zero backup*, or backing up the entire system as it stood the day that it was installed. For static systems that will not change much over the span of a year or two, this is helpful to do in the event that there is a catastrophic system failure.

Most administrators run incremental backups on weekday nights after normal operations and then full backups on a weekend night. Backup applications can easily be configured to run automatically; no one really needs to be present at the time of the backup. If a business runs 24/7, administrators choose times of low activity and run backups then. Some data might not be caught during the backup if there is a stateful session of data entry, but it will be caught during the next backup session; this situation might call for daily incremental and full backups.

Data can be backed up onto a variety of media, ranging from external hard drives—for the causal home user—to very expensive tape magnetic tape drives, usually the preferred media of data farms. Many small companies still use CD-RW or DVD-R disks, but this can be a cumbersome method. Smaller, less expensive DAT magnetic tape drives interface nicely with backup applications. Administrators run the backups during off hours or remotely and then simply make a physical tape change in the server room the next day. I customarily make full backups of a system I'm responsible for every day. This adds some expense to the tape budget, but I prefer magnetic tapes because the application interface assumes this media and the configuration of the backup rotation is easy.

Storing backups becomes a little tricky. Magnetic tapes last longer if they are stored in cool, dark, dry rooms that are under constant climate control. They don't last long if they are thrown in a box and stuffed in damp, overheated crawl spaces. Storing the data in secure rooms reduces the risk of theft. Imagine a company spending thousands of dollars monitoring for active data theft from a server and then throwing backup tapes into a drawer accessible to all employees.

It is possible to reduce data storage costs by decreasing the amount of data that goes to storage. Make sure that all parties know exactly which data must be stored. In addition to normal business operations, there are federal, state, and local regulations governing the storage of data, depending on the type of operation. Medical and student records must be stored and easily recoverable by governing bodies for a certain amount of time. Documents sensitive to police investigations must be stored for as long as the court indicates.

Chapter 14: Rotating Responsibilities and Auditing the Administrator

I have a friend with a wicked sense of humor. He has a degree in accounting. Instead of throwing crude, common expletives at each other, preferably while flashing the middle finger, we use a different expression. We look at each other and simply say, "Audit you."

A complete information security program mandates accountability. The user is accountable to the supervisor. The supervisor is accountable to the owner of the company, whether an individual or a board of directors. The board is accountable to the stockholders. The network administrator is ultimately accountable to every level of governance with no exceptions.

In a good security program, administrators rotate their responsibilities, especially as they pertain to accessing and protecting sensitive information. This rotation should become part of a regular audit of your network administrators. A network administrator is able to orchestrate events that are almost undetectable. Until he or she is thoroughly audited, these events may occur for years without any detection. The rotation of responsibilities can be planned or randomly applied, although the random method is best.

If there is a small IT department and rotation is not feasible, there are accounting firms that specialize in auditing IT administrators, systems, and processes. This is a different service from a security scan where the consultant may conduct an external penetration test or an internal access control test. Rather, the audit is specifically designed to determine if the network administrator is working to secure the network or participating in illicit or illegal practices using the company networking assets.

These practices are not perfect. It is possible for administrators, security officers, and auditors to collude and perpetrate crimes almost without detection. Also, auditing honest administrators can affect positive morale in the short run. No professional likes to think of his or herself as being under investigation. However, everyone is ultimately accountable and no one is above the law. If a system has allowed an administrator to operate with impunity, the opportunity for corruption increases.

Rotating responsibilities and auditing powerful administrators does not need to foster a climate of fear and retribution. Professionals understand accountability, as long as the concept is introduced in a professional, collegial manner. Where there is fear there will be lost productivity because people will spend time documenting and proving their innocence rather than working. However, to ignore the power of the network administrator, especially around sensitive and valuable information, is simply irresponsible.

Consider implementing a strategy called *segregation of duties*, which entails the same type of system as the control mechanisms in place for launching a nuclear weapon. Separate, unrelated individuals hold codes and physical keys, and those codes or keys must be entered in a precise order, which serves to ensure that there are no rogue elements unilaterally trying to start a nuclear war. In a network environment, multiple administrators would have varying responsibilities. One might be responsible for daily

104

log maintenance. One might have access to the data in the database, but not to the access control logs. Another might manage a log that records login attempts and data access attempts. This type of system is not intended to create snitches, but rather to reduce the opportunity for malicious behavior on the part of the administrators.

Most people do not want to be associated with illicit or illegal activity. They bring to the job an attitude of caring, professionalism, and diligence. Some weaker-willed individuals can maintain that attitude until they are in need and the opportunity for quick gain arises or until they are treated poorly and have total control of valuable electronic assets. There are sloppy, incompetent administrators who have complete control and fail to notice illegal activity, such as the person who allowed some pornography to go unnoticed on his server simply because he was too lazy to audit it. He served time for his laziness.

Good people can turn bad, and bad people will simply find opportunity. Managers do a service to employees by creating an environment that reduces opportunity for illicit and illegal activity. Creating a network environment where all are equally accountable and duties are rotated and segregated serves this purpose well.

Chapter 15: Designing the Adaptive and Scalable Enterprise Network

Assume for this chapter that the building your company will be occupying is merely a concept in the architect's mind, and that you have been invited to speak about issues pertaining to the computer network. The plan for the first year is to develop operations at this new location—headquarters—and then, over five years, to expand to five states and three countries. Within ten years, the corporation will be a truly global enterprise, but today, the architect has a sketchpad and needs some bright ideas from your team.

Spend some time focusing on the company's goals. Do you retail toys? Do you make bombs for the U.S. Air Force? Do you provide medical care to indigent peoples? Do you have the world's largest chain of discount department stores? Are you a research institute with a lot of intellectual property and the need to process complex calculations?

These divergent examples illustrate that computing needs are as divergent as these business types; therefore, the architecture of the system and the security needs are going to be equally divergent. Starting with a packaged solution simply will not work.

A television commercial several years ago about financial planning services claimed to offer customized solutions to fit individual's needs. The financial planner listened to a doctor describe his income and retirement needs, and suggested Plan A. The planner then listened to a grade-school teacher and gave her Plan B, and so on. I have seen too many prepackaged sales presentations from hardware and software vendors to know that they neither answer my questions nor respond individually to my needs.

On the other hand, I have been brought in to consult in situations where no real planning had taken place and a barely adequate network had been retrofitted as demand grew. One large social service organization implemented a metropolitan area network (MAN) after installing very different local area network (LAN) architectures in several satellite offices. While each unit manager was on board to unify the network, no planning had gone into the initial investment of hardware and software. The result was an expensive retrofit that did not function well.

There are philosophical differences driven by the peculiarities of business owners. One CEO of an investment company was adamant that the system be easy for him to use from home. Another business owner only cared about having cameras over the cash registers so that he could watch transactions taking place in his 15 locations. One director of a school required only that he could watch the hallways remotely from home to see if his instructors were adequately filling the students' time for all the required hours. None of these three decisions makers claimed to care a lot about the security of the systems, nor did they invest much time in guiding the process.

Differing opinions surround the effective design and security of large-scale, wide area networks. As technologies evolve, so do these opinions. Rather than recommend adoption of any one of these courses of action, they should be sorted out and applied to specific needs.

First and foremost, the system must serve the business needs of the organization, not the desires and fantasies of the network administrator. The data, services, and their security come first. Secondly, once the architecture serves the business model, it should be planned to adapt and scale up for growth. Buying network architecture for a projected five- or ten-year growth pattern is usually a waste of money. Good businesses adapt to the economy and to growth. They scale according to the movements of the economy. In the past, poor network planning and investments plagued the telecommunications industry. I know of buildings full of unused networking equipment. The business owners anticipated wild growth in landline telephone service and did not adapt to growth in cell phone use.

CENTRALIZED VS. DECENTRALIZED CONTROL

In a large, global WAN with multiple business units, the debate over centralized versus decentralized network management rages constantly. Large networks serving different business units within the same geographical area, such as a university, engage in this debate as well. Where the owner of the network stands on this issue will drive the design.

Centralized control usually consists of one main location of business servers for data storage, email, remote access services, Internet access, and other business functions. Remote locations might be equipped with authentication and print servers for local usage. With this extreme form of centralization, all applications are distributed and users are really working over a secure network on a server at the central location. The remote locations require very little administration. Users can be added remotely from the central office, and relatively inexperienced network personnel can manage print drivers either on- or off-site. In this model, data might be entered directly into central databases as users work, or it might be held in the remote server until the end of the workday and sent to the central location at night.

Working with distributed applications that enter data real time from the remote location into central databases might require the purchase of more bandwidth or dedicated bandwidth. The more people are using the application, the more bandwidth is required to speed up the process. If the data is entered and stored locally, a system will need to be designed to hold the data, back it up locally as required, and successfully transmit the data to the central databases at a specified time.

There are several benefits to centralized management if it serves the business needs of the organization:

- There is only one point of entry and filtering of Internet access.
- There is only one depository of data or centrally managed depositories of data.
- There is only one centrally managed security system for access controls, authentication, and monitoring.
- It gives you the ability to monitor and update workstations remotely from one location.

The disadvantages to centralized management include:

- The rigid system can be slow to respond to local needs.
- There is little or no local control of desktop applications.
- The larger the organization, the longer it takes to set up new employees.
- Local equipment failure or installation may require expensive outsourced services.
- The services offered to local users may be limited to the shared applications.

Decentralized control might entail a combination of several architectures and even different operating system platforms. The architecture can be as granular as every server being in a standalone LAN with a connecting backbone to all other LANs on the system. Each server would require a local administrator. An example of this might be a collection of independent networks connecting several small stores where each store is required to install and manage applications, maintain all data, administer any Internet connections, monitor all traffic, create user accounts, and repair/install all equipment locally.

The advantages of having total local control in a decentralized system include:

- Quick response to local issues, assuming that a qualified network administrator is on-site
- Independent operations that are responsive to local needs

- The ability to segregate networks and responsibilities so that no one network or person has control of all operations
- Localized management of security

The disadvantages are:
- Little or no sharing and, therefore, reduction in cost of system-wide services
- Isolated databases that would require consolidation
- Little control of organizational user policies
- Little or no ability to leverage system-wide purchases
- Fragmented and localized security monitoring

Somewhere in between these extremes is a combination of centralized and localized management that serves specific business needs. Let's look at how they could be applied to various business models.

In a privately owned school system with numerous campuses nationwide—where the curriculum and degree offerings are basically the same throughout—the centralized model may be a better fit. All the data gathered about students from enrollment through financial aid up to grades and, finally, granting a degree must be held in one central database. By federal law, this data must be secured so that no personal information about students can be accessible to anyone not having a legitimate role in the school.

By utilizing a system of centrally managed distributed applications, a student can get information about the school, apply for enrollment, apply for financial aid, drop/add courses, receive grades and new schedules, and graduate. Staff and faculty log into a system and launch the application interface. All details about the student's activity at the school are populating the central database in real time. The local network is easily managed mostly with remote access, but student assistance is utilized for local installation and maintenance. The local server is used for authentication and shared print drivers. This system is effective, yet with some downsides; some of the applications are not optimized for the system and can be irritatingly slow. Therefore, for some applications, data is held locally and sent directly to the central database at random times throughout the night. Nonetheless, in this instance, centralization works.

Think of two or three home-based networks in different houses. Each homeowner would buy, configure, and manage his own network. The owner of one house would typically not share network resources with the owners of the other houses. This setup is an example of a decentralized system.

What should be clear now is that the owner of a networked system can have as much or as little centralized control as he or she needs to suit the business type. In the past, only the very large and wealthy corporations could afford to implement any distributed but centrally managed services—and even these were arcane in comparison to what is now available—but it is becoming more common even for small- to medium-sized businesses to be able to implement a centralized system.

SYSTEM INFRASTRUCTURE

The chosen management model for the system's architecture will dictate the infrastructure of the data communications, meaning the bandwidth required. At one time, connecting networks was limited to the bandwidth provided by using the telephone service. The network architecture was subservient to available bandwidth. Now, systems architects have a wide variety of data communications to plan around and implement, selecting the appropriate bandwidth after the most suitable architecture is chosen.

Cost may be a limiting factor. Once an architecture has been chosen, the appropriate bandwidth may not make economic sense. The architects must then revisit the plan and produce a balanced system that satisfies data delivery needs and budget constraints. The architects develop an adaptive scalable plan that allows them to roll out more services across the system as bandwidth becomes more cost-effective.

HARDWARE INFRASTRUCTURE

In my past administrative roles, I was inundated with advertising for muscle hardware; no matter what the size of the enterprise I was associated with, I received advertising for bigger, faster, more powerful hardware. Many architects simply waste money in this area. Instead of starting with consideration for the business model and planning an adaptive and scalable system around it, they begin with hardware. Very often I see expensive hardware serving a handful of users when it was designed to handle thousands of remote users and terabytes of data. If there is money to burn in an IT department, it unfortunately ends up being spent on unnecessary hardware.

A few years ago, I worked as a consultant for a 20-person graphic design startup. During my initial tour, the CEO bragged that he had spent over $500,000 on a network. I immediately recommended that they shed much of the unused networking equipment and instead upgrade the graphics workstations. I offered a network design that was scalable to five cities, was mostly centrally controlled, and offered a unique opportunity for clients to meet remotely in real time with the designers. If the CEO had sold half the equipment, the startup could have upgraded the workstations, increased the bandwidth, and scaled up as needed. The owner instead chose to buy even more equipment and bandwidth in order to have all five cities fully functional. Not surprisingly, the company went broke.

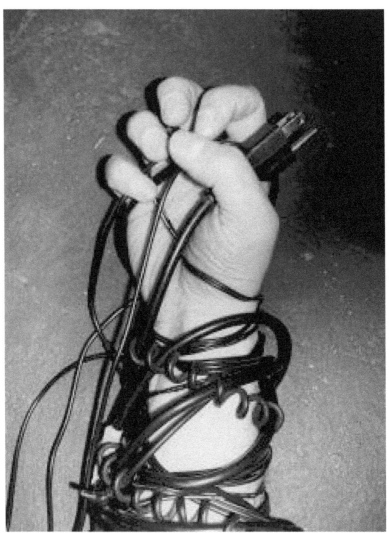
Photo by Matt Rohrbach

Part II
Internet Safety

Section I
How the Internet Works

INTRODUCTION

What is commonly referred to as the Internet is a complex system of interconnected computers, many of them housing information easily accessible to almost any other computer. The Internet allows for real-time 'virtual' communication between individuals. People can exchange anything from basic emails to high-quality sound and video, and see and hear many individuals simultaneously. These connections can be with friends and family or with perfect strangers. Almost everyone has a story about a stranger trying to make unsolicited or unwanted contact over the Internet. Horror stories abound of convicted sex offenders and other evildoers using the Internet to hunt down victims. Therefore, anyone who accesses a social or dating website such as Match.com or Facebook should be aware of the potential risks of this form of socializing and proceed with caution.

The accessibility to information that the Internet offers is great for children. Websites such as Disney.com, Discovery.com, and Thehistorychannel.com are family-safe and offer valuable, entertaining information suitable for any age. Unfortunately, by being on the Internet, children are at-risk to exposure to inappropriate content such as pornography, sites that promote racism, religious intolerance, or hate, and chat rooms where nefarious strangers with ulterior motives lurk.

The Internet also presents a whole host of software and technical problems. Innocently downloading free information and entertainment can be a vehicle to invite viruses, spyware, rootkits, and other types of malware onto a computer's hard drive. These can ruin your data, spy on your computer, and even steal personal information, which can then lead to identity theft. Some sites offering downloadable movies, music, books, and other media may, in fact, even be illegal for distributing copyrighted content.

In this way, the Internet is a double-edged sword: It offers a means of gaining access to information that might otherwise be out of reach to millions and it is the optimal mode of free speech, using blogs, e-newsletters, video clips, and any other media supported on the Internet, but the mechanics of the Internet are such that it was developed to be precise, not private. Individual users need to protect their identity and privacy proactively; the Internet will not do it for them. The governance of the Internet has never been about censorship of any kind. While there are laws in many countries pertaining to certain types of information that can be hosted, shared, or viewed on the Internet, they are not consistent; what is illegal and reviled in one country is perfectly acceptable in another. Users need to plan a strategy for making this magnificent tool safe to use.

Automobile manufacturers are expected to make a car safe to drive; they can be sued for failure to do so. Congress even dictates minimum safety standards. For many years, the Internet was not governed. What little amount of governance exists today affects only a small group of people placing information online. Some laws are local, some are national, and a few are international, but then only a few countries accept and recognize them. Internet users cannot wait for their government to intervene and protect their privacy or prevent predators and identify thieves from victimizing them. Users must be aware and proactive of the potential risks in an effort to avoid becoming victims.

The notion that only children are victims on the Internet is both naïve and wrong. Revealing child predators is laudable but often overshadows—and therefore seems to minimize—the risks to all other potential victims. Anyone can be a potential victim of someone using the Internet as the vehicle for abuse, and therefore, Internet safety should be examined with all users in mind.

The Internet is a great tool for communication and information. Using this tool safely requires an education on the technology of the Internet, an understanding of how this technology can be used by perpetrators, and strategies for avoiding risks of all kinds.

Chapter 16: The Internet and the World Wide Web

Understanding the basics of networking covered in chapter 1 is the first step toward completely understanding, and therefore having more control of, Internet use. The Internet is safer when the user is in control.

To further our understanding and control of the Internet, it's important to clearly define what the Internet is. The terms "Internet" and "the Web," a shortened version of the World Wide Web (www), are mistakenly used synonymously when they are actually very different.

THE INTERNET

Common and simplistic definitions simply tell us that the Internet is many thousands, perhaps millions, of computers interconnected. If that's all it was, the Internet as we know it would not work. Also, the history of the Internet is often glossed over with a snappy bit about ARPANET, the so-called model-T of the Internet, developed by the Department of Defense. Actually, the concept and basic technologies of the Internet preceded the development of ARPANET by almost a decade. There is no precise "first" inventor of the Internet; scientists in education and government knew they could break data into packets and wanted a method of sending that packetized data to other computers. Major universities developed local intranets for sending data between departments and the military funded research that ultimately lead to unified standards for data transmission rates, modems, packet sizes, transmission protocols, and transmission infrastructures such as telephone lines.

It is fairly simple to understand why scientists picked the plain, old telephone system as the transmission infrastructure; it was there. The also understood that data was simply ones and zeros. They needed two things to make the initial concept work: a method for breaking data into manageable sizes that would transmit across telephone lines and a way of converting the digital signals into analog signals, and then converting them back so the computer could deal with the digital data. The protocols were written that created the packets and the modem was invented to convert the data from digital to analog and then back again.

The packets, as explained in chapter 1, needed to be numbered and addressed and the developers of these protocols had no need to make these anonymous or to delete them completely when no longer necessary. This resulted in a system that exactly identifies the computer the data comes from and the computer the data is going to, and this is indelible. While it can take some work to find the source computer of illegal activity, it can inevitably be found. The recipient computer will also be found. This important concept will be useful several times throughout this book. The Internet was developed to be precise, not private.

When there were 200 to 300 computers interconnected in the original manifestations of the "Internet," the addressing and routing was fairly simplistic. As more computers were added, a system needed to be developed to route data as precisely and efficiently as when there were just a few computers. The data still had to get to the exact computer and not to every computer. When people refer to the "millions of interconnected computers" they are really referring to this system. Computers were connected to the Internet that contained the data about various computers in a certain area and when an inquiry was made regarding a certain address, these computers were polled to determine where the requested computer was located and when it was found, the data was sent to that exact computer. The idea is simple: Remember where a specific address is located and send the data to it. This infrastructure, once it became sophisticated enough to handle a greater complexity of computers, was the technology that allowed the World Wide Web to function.

The other key concept to understanding the Internet is this: The data sent over the Internet goes from the source computer and is then routed through any number of servers. These servers add addresses to packet headers en route. Therefore, not only are the source and destination well known, but the route the data takes across the system is also known. All of the computers are designed to stamp the data with the date and time, which is also indelible.

It is possible to spoof or mask addressing of source and destination computers, but unless the user knows every server administrator who colludes with them in this process and can accurately predict every server the data will pass through, the route is known and remains indelible.

The same concept applies to more modern transmission infrastructures such as cable, fiber optic, and satellite. When a user sends data, the medium of travel doesn't matter; the addressing identifying the computer, the route traveled, and the date and time of the transmission are clear for any administrator to see. When some of the topics regarding risk and prevention are covered, it will be helpful to return to this concept.

When giving basic security lectures to networking students, I enjoyed the numerous attempts at trying to consider how to mask the identifying data. Students first think of removing the network interface card containing the media access control (MAC) address. They quickly learn how Internet protocol addresses can be spoofed. There are also methods that allow a computer to appear to be in a different part of the world. These are all used by perpetrators of illegal activity to attempt to hide their activity and real identity—and some are actually good enough at it to stay ahead of the police for several years. However, this is a temporary mask and the true identity of the perpetrator can be found. Moving off shore or to a country where certain laws do not apply is another choice people wishing to perpetrate illegal activity over the Internet make.

The Internet is the conduit for the exchange of data types such as email. An application is written that organizes the email, works with the computer to packetize it, and then a protocol that exists on the sending and receiving computers allows the email to pass across the Internet and be opened at the recipient computer. Email was used very extensively prior to the introduction of the Web, just as many other methods for communicating such as file transfer protocol (FTP) and the bulletin board systems (BBS). These communication tools did not utilize web pages or portals; they were direct links established between the computers using data transfer protocols.

THE WORLD WIDE WEB

The creation of what we now take for granted, the display of information and the interactivity within a web page that allows us to do such things as book a flight or pay bills online, is attributed to a Swiss physicist Tim Berners-Lee. In 1992, he thought it would be great if he could display research papers electronically and link one paper to another for quick reference. The result is the 10 billion web pages mentioned at the beginning of this book.

The primary objective was to display and link information. At first, the goal was to display text and then, as the underlying tagging system hypertext markup language (HTML) evolved, complex graphics could be displayed as well. However, to move from a static display environment where the user had no interactivity with the website to the dynamic sites we take for granted today required further evolution of HTML and the integration of scripting languages such as Visual Basic, PHP, Perl, and others. Programs were written that allowed Internet users to send and receive information.

The Web uses the infrastructure of the Internet through distributed name services (DNS). A web server uses a static or unchangeable IP address. A website owner buys or rents a uniform resource locator (URL), which is the name of the website such as yahoo.com. If the website owner also owns the static IP address, he or she can host the site from his or her home or business. Most companies choose to rent space on a web server. Once the URL is registered, it is associated in one of the many computers on the Internet with a static IP address where the website sits. When you try to find a specific website, you do not need to know the IP address; just the URL or website name. Your query is directed to the host computer once this association between the URL and IP address is propagated through the databases on the Internet.

This is good to know when trying to track down the owner of a website or trying to find where the website is being hosted. The invention of the World Wide Web was brilliant and changed forever our methods of communicating. However, once you take a four-hour class in HTML, buy a URL, and host your site, you can say almost anything you like true or not. If a website makes a false promise or contains derogatory yet false information about someone, the owner of the URL can be looked up and the company that issued the URL will have a record of the website owner, webmaster, contact information, and— normally—where the site is being hosted. Finding the website owners is the easy part. Getting them to take the false information down requires a formal process that will be discussed later. Moreover, if the site contains illegal content or if the website owner is using the site to steal information, media, merchandise, or funds, the local police may not be able to intervene. The issue may be serious enough that they will put their resources on the case to assist in finding out which jurisdiction is responsible for investigating and prosecuting the crime, or they may not. The website owner may be sitting in a boat in the middle of the Atlantic Ocean and the website host can be in a country where the activity is not illegal. Nevertheless, if you can ascertain the jurisdiction of the website owner and/or host, report it to their police. If you can't, and the matter is serious enough, report it locally and see if the local authorities and resources can help. While there are some things local laws will not allow on a website, false information needs to be proactively corrected.

For our purposes, this level of understanding of how the Internet and the World Wide Web function will help us approach the following subjects more easily.

Chapter 17: Search Engines, Web Browsers, and Internet Service Providers

No person or corporation owns the World Wide Web, but a few corporations own the backbone of the Internet. The interconnected networks that make up the Internet are owned by major telecommunications companies like Verizon, Quest, and AT&T. They sell access by wholesale quantities to smaller companies who become local or regional Internet service providers (ISPs). The major telecoms are also in the business of providing consumer and business level Internet access. Whether it is a dial-up, cable, or satellite connection, this is simply access to a vast network.

Many ISPs double as web-hosting or co-locating facilities. Not only do they give consumers access to the WWW, but they also sell space on their servers where website owners can upload and manage their sites.

If a child accidentally or even intentionally views obscene material, a law is potentially broken. In the United States, it is illegal to give access to pornographic material to anyone under the age of 18. Some webmasters create ubiquitous warning and opt out pages that are launched when their URL is hit. The person viewing the page must proactively accept access to the site or leave. There is rarely a verification process to determine the actual age of the viewer. The question remains: Who is responsible if the child proceeds to the pornographic material?

Many might argue the parents or guardians of the child are ultimately responsible. Some might argue the ISP is responsible for allowing access to these sites. Still others would argue the webmaster/owner who created the site and does nothing to control access to legal aged adults is to blame.

This argument is at the very core of all further consideration of Internet safety. If my elderly mother becomes a victim of fraud on an Internet-based auction site, is the auction site responsible? What if the auction site did not screen the persons or companies trying to sell products on their website and allowed convicted felons to perpetrate theft? There is little doubt who would be held legally accountable if someone creates an adult content website and intentionally markets access to it to children. The waters become muddied when it comes to issues revolving around sites with legitimate and legal content that are used by others to perpetrate a crime.

Many sites are now created specifically for the purpose of sending viruses, spybots, and rootkits (more one these later) to site visitors. Informationweek.com reports that there are now nearly 30,000 new malicious sites popping up every day.

If ISPs were to be held responsible for monitoring threats, hate, scams, fraud, and any other illegal type of Internet activity many would simply close their doors; the cost of monitoring all Internet traffic is too huge. The bottom line is fairly simple: Until the issue of ISP responsibility is completely resolved, do not expect ISPs to do much about making your Internet experience a safe one. While they may advertise programs they offer to assist customers, the ultimate responsibility still lies with the user. These value-added services are often very useful for educating children and restricting access to certain sites, but the ISPs offer them for marketing purposes and still see themselves as conduits, not regulators.

It is possible to monitor traffic at the ISP level but, as previously noted, is very expensive. When the police are investigating cyber-crimes, they have the ability to subpoena any person or entity between the source of the crime and the victim if they feel there is evidence to be gathered. ISPs routinely work with police by providing traffic logs and can even go so far as to duplicate downloads and file transfer across their networks. The exact process of gathering and preserving cyber evidence is worthy of a book in itself. For our purposes here, we will suffice with the concept that while it is possible to shift the responsibility for maintaining perfectly safe web surfing experiences onto the ISP, it is not going to happen anytime soon. The responsibility, then, falls on the user.

THE WEB BROWSER

One of the best places for a user to begin to make the Internet a safe place to visit is the first point of entry, the browser. Most people accept the industry default browser, Internet Explorer. This is a Microsoft product that is usually packaged with various operating systems. Nevertheless, this is not the only browser available. There are others that work on any Microsoft operating system such as Netscape, Firefox, and Google Chrome.

There had been some contention that ultimately led to various lawsuits regarding the compatibility of other browsers with the Microsoft family of operating systems.

135

This is not the place for a lengthy discussion on that topic, but it is good to know that the creators of other web browsers approach their product development in their own way and the result may be some lack of compatibility.

What is common for all web browsers is the vulnerability. The browser is the tool used to search for the unique URL, or the website name. This search can be aided by a search engine or a service such as Google that indexes website names and is capable of matching content searches with URLs. The browser connects to the search engine and the web search is on. It is not necessary to use Google or any other search engine. The user can simply write the URL in the address line at the top of the web browser interface and the requested site will appear.

The potential risk becomes fairly obvious. Children can, when unattended, type any words they choose into a search engine and websites with that kind of content will be listed. They can scroll down the list, sometimes 200,000 deep, and open almost any of these websites.

The result can be children exposed to content parents do not want them to see, which is usually what gets parents excited the most. It is so easy for a browser and search engine to deliver inappropriate content for certain age groups. Various content filters have been developed and some are more successful than others. Libraries have experimented with them but they found the filters blocked too much acceptable research content and, therefore, they usually abandoned the filtering system and instead opt now to post a warning to users not to view certain types of content or risk losing computing privileges or, worse, have their activity investigated by police.

Children aside, accessing legitimate content still poses a risk to the user. I have long tried to understand the reason people will attach viruses to website content knowing the people who visit the site will potentially infect their computers. I have listened to lectures by criminal justice professors as they attempt to explain the "cracker" mentality and, after fairly extensive research, my best conclusion is no one really knows why. They can point to some crackers who are angry, some who are greedy and want your credit card information and some who are simply sinister at heart and delight in wrecking your computer. There is no one reason, however, therefore making it nearly impossible to predict what type of site a cracker may choose to plant the virus or spybot.

There is an option in most browsers to limit or restrict certain websites, and then to mark some websites as trusted. This is good practice within a corporation that wants employees to have access to internal information or production websites but then wants to limit access to most sites on the external Web. This can also be done at home. We will discuss strategies that focus specifically on this later. My intent in this discussion of web browsers is that while functionality exists in many browsers, it may still not result in a perfectly safe experience.

The most effective strategy for Internet safety is not a technical solution; it is not an application that only finds safe sites. The solution does not lie in the computer but rather in the user. The user controls the computer and should put his or her self into a position to control the content viewed on the Internet. The issue of safe surfing with children is not an easy one to address until a parent, guardian, or designated adult is sitting with them when they look for websites. If there is no supervision, then the computer can be turned off. This is a low-tech solution; use the on and off button. With that as the ultimate starting point, what follows is further clarification and an explanation of Internet technologies as well as a refinement of the premise that the user is in control and responsible for making the Internet a safe place to go.

Chapter 18: Securing Financial Transactions Over the Internet

To understand how most financial transactions are vulnerable to cracking, let's look at a common and easily understood architecture used for completing certain types of transactions. Banks and other online retailers may very well customize this process, but the concept is pretty universal and the architecture detailed here is fairly common.

The vulnerabilities will vary between transaction infrastructures, as will the methods used for encrypting the information containing account numbers, dollar figures, and transaction receipts. The underlying technologies for this explanation are Perl within a common gateway interface (CGI) on a Linux hosting platform.

Perl 6.0 is one of the most robust and flexible programming languages for creating a CGI in commercial-grade websites and portals. Using a CGI on a Linux platform offers webmasters both stability and speed, and Perl is a natural fit as a programming language. While this chapter will focus on the use of Perl for creating CGI, this programming language is preferred as well for network management on the Linux platform.

THE PERL PROGRAMMING LANGUAGE

Perl is considered a high-level scripting language much like C++, Visual Basic, Java Script and PHP. The syntax of this type of language is familiar to most people. Commonly the

"*If* (this condition exists) *then* (this action will occur)" statement is written in plain English. The condition can be a comparison of monetary values when calculating exchange rates (If $x = 1$ euro then $y = 1.34825$ USD), or a simple comparison of arithmetic values to determine a mortgage payment.

High-level scripting languages differ from machine or assembler languages. These are written closer to the binary required to make a computer function. The high-level scripting languages are intended to be easy to write and are then converted to binary using either a compiler or an interpreter.

C++ and Visual Basic programs use a compiler and are permanently converted to binary and saved as executable programs. Languages such as Perl and PHP are interpreted, which means they remain in the form of the original scripting language and are converted only when the program is actually needed, then converted back to the script.

There are specific uses for both compiled and interpreted programs. Perl and PHP programmers like the speed and efficiency they enjoy when using an interpreter. When a program is compiled, many lines of code are attached to the program and while the actual performance of the functions is fast, the execution is slow. Interpreted programs initiate faster and are, therefore, useful when, for instance, numerous batch files need to be run. Many network administrators write automated tools in both Perl and PHP simply because they use less of the server resources when batch processing.

This is a serious consideration when creating CGI script.

COMMON GATEWAY INTERFACE (CGI)

Interpreted languages are commonly used in websites or portals to process financial transactions or to update user information. These can be programmed to run as a batch process of many individual transactions at once, or processed individually in real time. The most common application of CGI is for processing online transactions. The buyer fills out an interactive form, selects the item to buy, provides a credit card number, and waits as the program submits the request.

Many things can then take place automatically that will expedite the purchase. First, the program can search a database to see if the buyer is already a customer. If so, there could be a validation process to verify the information about the buyer and all of the customer information can be called automatically and used to expedite the transaction. Finally the CGI script can send the order to the warehouse, fulfill the order, and inform all parties when the order ships.

The functions of the program are ultimately determined by the specifics needs of marketing, finance, product management, and fulfillment. Each online retailer will have specific needs, but there are packaged online retail programs available that are easily customized for different specific needs. When creating a CGI, the programming language used must be fast and accurate. Perl is an excellent choice for this purpose.

THE LINUX PLATFORM

Among competing operating systems, the one that stands out for hosting websites and portals is Linux. This is true also for DNS look ups, one of the most common functions of the World Wide Web. While Microsoft is working diligently to overcome Linux/UNIX in supporting Internet functions, Linux remains the most commonly used.

There are a few reasons Linux is the choice of webmasters and site owners. It is a free, open-source platform that is easily and efficiently managed. Linux administrators typically use command line interface (CMI) to administer web hosting servers. This allows them to bypass slow graphical user interfaces (GUIs). This speeds up the process of moving or updating data. Ultimately, with CMIs, processes and data management are much easier to control.

Linux is a logical environment rather than a physical one, and many of the functions are intuitive and done once. More importantly, the directory structure of a logical architecture allows for faster transfer of data. A logical directory structure can be more easily explained through demonstration. For example, a webmaster might need to move 60 gigabytes of content from a directory accessed by a content editor to the website. In a physical directory structure, the data moves up and then down the hierarchy of the directories, files, and folders. In a logical environment, the data moves straight across from one directory to another.

This architecture allows an interpreted language such as Perl to call the interpreter, which can be located anywhere in the Linux directory structure, initiate the CGI script, move the data, and close the program faster than in any of the competing physical architectures.

SECURING ONLINE TRANSACTIONS

Using Perl as a CGI script in a Linux environment offers the webmaster a fast and reliable method of handling data input. As a user, however, we want to know that the program taking our financial data is secure. There are a few things to look for when entering data into an online retailer to buy Christmas gifts.

First, programmers are advised when they write CGI script to ensure that the script does what it was intended to do. The line that takes your name does only that. The line that takes your order does only that. The line that takes your credit card number and validates it does only that. You should see some kind of action when you enter the data such as 'Checking the database for your information,' 'Checking stock to see if your item is in,' or 'Verifying credit card.' If you start to see responses from the website that are not directly associated with the data you just entered, or if you see no response, chances are the programmer did not think of security when writing the CGI script. Make a point of contacting the retailer and asking for an explanation of their CGI script security.

Secondly, stay clear of available options to remember your data, especially your credit card number and address. While this function speeds up the processing time of an order, you are giving permission for your data to be stored on another computer. If you trust the site and really want to use this option, then at least take the time to read their security and privacy policies. If you do not see an explanation of how this data is secured, contact the retailer and ask.

This chapter was designed to give you some understanding of the mechanics of online transactions. It is worthy to note that law enforcement has this same understanding of these types of transactions and they are very careful to ensure the integrity of the technology as they conduct investigations of any kind involving fraud, theft, possession and transfer of illegal pornography, and harassment. Later in this book we will examine methods and steps the web developer and user can take to also help ensure the integrity and security of each transaction. Nevertheless, keep in mind that in spite of our best efforts to conceal the content of a transaction, the Internet activity itself is precise and not necessarily private. We can usually protect credit card numbers and personal data from potential thieves, but the history of the actual transaction is always accessible to the ISP and law enforcement authorities with proper credentials.

Chapter 19: Virtual Communities: Chat Rooms, Social Sites, and Blogs

I am an avid cyclist and belong to a virtual community where I can boast about my long rides. I upload the routes and, perhaps, even the profiles, and I know many of the members of the community are slightly exaggerating their accomplishments just as I do, but that's part of the fun of it. By sharing information about routes and conditions, I am able to plan my weekend rides a little better.

When I joined this virtual community, my intent was to use it as a marketing vehicle for my book on cycling. I requested permission to use their web portal for this purpose and they agreed. I even got some prime space up front to promote the book. I discovered, however, that I got more out of the community if I just did what the community was designed for: describe my rides, track my mileage, and share information with other cyclists.

I am acutely aware of the potential risks of putting my name and personal information on a website for others to see. No doubt much of the spam mail I get comes from the few sites where my email address is visible. Nevertheless, I take this with a grain of salt and equate it to watching television, where I am inundated with advertising I don't like and a lot of content that is, at best, silly. Therefore, I consider the type of content in the virtual community and the likelihood of someone completely distrustful finding my personal data and abusing it.

The more pernicious attackers who would want to deposit spybots and rootkits on to your computer will do so through popular sites. This includes every type of website and virtual community. It is very common to find this activity in file sharing sites where individuals make available unlicensed or copied programs. Along with the free graphic design applications come the viruses, rootkits, and spybots. I don't have much sympathy for someone whose computer is infected as they try to steal from a legitimate software development company.

The risks of joining and regularly visiting a virtual community are primarily the exposure of your personal data to abuse and your computer to varieties of malicious code. The underlying technology that allows this to happen is easy to understand.

When someone joins a virtual community, there is typically a profile page where the new member enters the kind of data that is designed to encourage other members to converse or share information with them. Some communities are better than others at hiding personal data and making it accessible only to other members, others do a terrible job. There is typically an option for a new member to not enter any personal data at all, thereby diminishing the potential of sharing with others. Some more sophisticated sites allow new members to hide information from the public. Regardless of the options, there are programs run by persons wishing to obtain personal data, whether for illicit or legitimate purposes, that scan every portion of the community for email addresses, phone numbers, names associated with these, and any other personal data they can acquire. It is easy to become a new member and then scan the site for this data.

Social Sites have become increasingly popular; millions of people join, create elaborate personalized sites, and interconnect with friends, family, and often complete strangers. Facebook, Friendster, and MySpace are just a few of these types of sites. The risk of joining these sites was immediately recognized; all kinds of predators join and track down the type of person they want to victimize. They often hide their identity behind fake names or block other members from viewing their identity. They track down their victims and try to make personal contact. Mostly it is the young who are prey to this type of cyber stalking.

These social sites make an attempt to assist families, law enforcement, and potential victims by allowing for special safeguards to prevent predators from finding them. If a known predator is an active member, these sites attempt to help law enforcement track them down. While this is a noble attempt, it is often flawed. If young people are savvy enough to know they can lie on their application to the site and circumvent the age restrictions, predators can certainly lie, too. In one notorious case, a 19-year-old man presented himself as16 on a social website. A 13-year-old girl lied about her age as well, indicating she was 16 also. The two got together, had sex, and the 19-year-old was charged with statutory rape.

A recent incident involved a young girl looking for acceptance and a mother of another neighbor girl. The mother created a social site profile pretending to be a young boy interested in the girl. The mother, posing as the boy, led the girl to believe he was in love with her and then suddenly turned on the girl with vile insults and humiliation. The young girl hanged herself in her closet.

It should go without saying that parents should closely monitor their child's activity on these social sites and should actively involve themselves in the interactions their children have with other members of the site. The security personnel at these sites are happy to help when there is trouble.

BLOGS

I write a biweekly blog on information security. The link to that blog site will be found in the appendix of this book listing Internet links of interest. The most interesting aspect of writing for the Internet is not only the sheer amount of information available through blog sites, but also that it is an almost unrestricted venue. I try to follow some reasonable journalistic principles when I write. First, if I cannot personally verify the information, I usually don't include it—especially if it questions the character of another human being. Second, if someone presents me with wild conspiracy theories, I take a quick look and try to find some factual verification of the theory. Failing that, I ignore the information. Finally, if I adhere to and promote a technical process, I have tried it first.

A quick read of many popular blogs will reveal these principles are not always followed. Many entertaining blogs, which—in all fairness—are not meant to be serious information, are nothing more than whimsical musings. Some are outright lies. Finally, some are dark conspiracy theories meant to discredit a government official, religion, or even a country.

In between emails and blogs, teenagers use a variety of venues to communicate about each other. The most notorious of these are websites, email bombs, and text messages that tell outright lies about another teenager or reveal embarrassing yet very confidential information. This type of cyber bullying grows every day as teenagers become more and more savvy and inventive.

The world of the wiki, or websites that allow visitors to change or alter information, has served as one of the primary tools for this activity. High school teachers and college professors hold suspect information in a student paper obtained from the wiki site. Anyone can write anything they like. Most recently, large corporations with questionable practices have been discovered altering information about themselves in so-called independent wiki sites. The most pernicious use of wiki sites is when teenagers gang up on one of their peers and several different students pile on the insults and harassment. While states and school districts struggle to adopt effective legislation and policies to crack down on bullying in light of the nationwide attention the 2010 suicide of Irish exchange student Phoebe Prince as a result of bullying garnered, the Internet remains a wide open technological playground that students can use in lieu of good old fashioned fact-to-face bullying.

In the semi-controlled world of website management, there are procedures in place for requesting the "Take Down" of false or copyrighted information. This is a small consolation to the teenager who is viciously attacked by peers. Dealing with cyber bullying is a subject to be covered later in this book.

CHAT ROOMS

Chat rooms are nothing more than an expanded version of Instant Messaging. Using basically the same protocols and very simple interfaces, visitors to websites can join a conversation that is taking place between any number of people from any number of countries. Few chat rooms exercise any kind of control over who is allowed to enter. "Joining" a chat room is often as easy as entering a username. Most participants know enough not to use their own name. It is accepted that this masking is often necessary to conceal personal identity, but it is also accepted this is a practice used by predators. Not many people would willingly chat with a violent, angry sex offender, but if that predator can mask himself behind the face of a kindly, generous person, he is going to get more response.

The popular television program *To Catch a Predator* highlighted the unseemly world of predators using chat rooms to lure or connect with underage children for sex. Their practice of using adults who enter into chat rooms as children has come under some scrutiny, but the outcome has been the arrest and conviction of adults who make the connection in a chat room and boldly declare they want to have sex with children.

While chat rooms and websites were not invented for this purpose, the most common perception among Internet users is that this is the most frequently cited reason for using a chat room. I use Instant Messaging between myself and the people I know and trust, but I immediately understood that I could not actually identify any of the participants in chat rooms and, therefore, I don't join in their conversations.

CONCLUSION

The notion of using cyber space to meet people is at first intriguing but reality quickly sets in. I far prefer to meet someone new in a public environment such as a coffee shop, restaurant, or my workplace. I like the advertisement where a sweating scam artist is trying to pass a wrinkled, phony certified check off to an individual in a coffee shop. From outward appearances, we know it's a scam. In a chat room or social site, if scam detectors are not being used to their fullest, it is easier to think the people we meet there are perfectly reliable and trustworthy.

These communication tools have value and are good for their intended purpose of bringing people from all corners of the world together. However, it is imperative to understand how they can be abused. Later, we will examine and build strategies for their safe use.

Chapter 20: The Future of the Internet: Improvements and Challenges

Previous chapters attempted to explain the underlying technologies through examples of use. The risks these technologies bring are easier to comprehend when we see how they can be used for good and also be abused.

IMPROVEMENTS

Going forward, there are two significant changes that Internet users will experience in the next few years. First, there will be significant increases in bandwidth, allowing ever more complex content to be delivered. (I no longer refer to content as being displayed on the Internet, it is delivered.) Most information today is delivered in the form of professionally edited audio and video segments and programs.

Bandwidth will only increase in the future. Most universities are connected to what is referred to as Internet2, a very high-speed network of fiber optics. With this increase in bandwidth comes the increased ability to deliver content.

The second most important change to the Internet is the introduction of new IP addressing known as IPv6, or Internet protocol version 6. Currently, the Internet uses an IP addressing model that uses four octets of three numbers (IPv4). There are so many devices connecting to the Internet it was feared that we would run out of IPv4 addresses. IPv6 uses a longer alphanumeric series theoretically allowing some 340,282,366,920,938,463, 463,374,607,431,768,211,456 electronic objects to use an IP address and connect to the Internet. If you are good with math, that means, theoretically, there are 6.67×10^{27} IP addresses for every square yard of earth space.

I have used my cell phone to read email, but rarely. I enjoy watching people who seem to be addicted to electronic information and are reading their handheld Internet devices everywhere. With IPv6, any electronic device that can display or deliver data or content can be connected to the Internet, including the chip they planted in my cat. It is not farfetched to think I could track where my cat is on the Internet.

CHALLENGES

It would be easy to write alarming predictions of potential abuse of these technologies by government entities, private corporations, and other individuals. What specifically they might do is good fodder for novels and movies, but it is always possible. In his novel *1984,* George Orwell predicted technology capable of allowing Big Brother to place cameras in every home and observe every human movement. I have spent a little time considering the opinions of some conspiracy theorists simply because I know it is technologically—if not politically—possible to place a camera inside every home in our country. Think about the available webcams located in ski areas, along bicycle and driving routes, and in other public places.

I helped organize a student project for students in a criminal justice program that developed an interactive map of security cameras in a small suburb of Seattle. The general notion was to make this data base of security cameras available to the local police so in the event of a crime, they could determine if the act was caught on one of the numerous security cameras throughout the city. At face value, this is a very easy project to sign up for; the local police are always underfunded and need all the help they can get. If they can get a tape containing the actual crime, their lives are so much easier. I helped advise the project to completion with the sobering knowledge someone could develop a similar project for nefarious reasons. For example, anyone who has access to these cameras in real time or to the archived tapes can use them to intrude on the privacy of individuals and even detect behavior patterns that would give them sufficient information to burglarize a home or business without detection.

I also observed with concern the reports of the government in Myanmar limiting or completely eliminating Internet connections during their period of unrest in September of 2007. When one studies the map of the various interconnected networks of the Internet (http://advice.cio.com/themes/CIO.com/cache/Internet_ma p_labels_0.pdf), it is not difficult to imagine taking down or controlling the Internet in the United States. There are a few very large players who control the majority of these networks. While the Internet has become a magnificent tool for expressing free speech and sharing information quickly, it is necessary to keep an eye on developments that might serve to control access and content.

We know very little about what the Internet will be like in 20 years. Regardless of developments, it will always present challenges. Those who will thrive have a vision for this information revolution that will serve the good, but the improvements in capacity and ability over the Internet will only increase the potential abuse.

As the next section moves into specific issues of risk, these chapters on the technological underpinnings of the Internet will be referred to as necessary.

Section II
Potential Risks of Internet Use

Chapter 21: How Children are at Risk:
Exposure, Exploitation, and Addiction

This chapter will take on some special considerations for the safety of children who use the Internet. It is divided into three categories.

First, the greatest risk family's face when allowing children to use the Internet is exposure to material that is not age appropriate or that is just simply morally unacceptable to the entire family. This could be pornography, but could also include violent or racist content.

Second, there is the risk of being exploited by online predators, and this presents some very obvious risks, such as being lured away from home. There is also the risk of the child being tempted to misuse the Internet in many ways, some of which are criminal, in exchange for money and gifts.

Finally, one of the risks often overlooked for any age group, but especially for preteen and teenage children is addiction. It is not the intent or scope of this book to examine Internet addiction in any authoritative way, but only to examine recent statistics and symptoms. From there, parents and children should seek out the assistance of health care professionals if they believe there is a problem.

EXPOSURE
For anyone who has raised or been around young children for any length of time, it is obvious that the brain progressively develops from an infantile state to full mature

159

adulthood. The level of "maturity" is often relative, but most children progress toward adulthood in a predictable pattern. Some children are slightly ahead or behind others. I remember sometimes being exposed to information that was often thought to be a bit beyond my years. My sixth grade teacher caught me reading *The Catcher in the Rye,* a book ordinarily assigned to ninth grade students. She asked me pointed questions about the characters, plot, subplots, and significance of the title. I was not entirely versed in the subtle nuances a freshman in high school would be led through, but she was satisfied that I could grasp the material and did not take the book away.

For the most part, it's up to parents to decide what their children should be exposed to. I often disagree, but the law favors the parent. The law has also decided upon learned advice that children and adolescents under the age of 18 do not have the ability to comprehend the subtle nuances of pornography. I agree.

The law requires purveyors of pornography on the Internet to warn and caution visitors of the site that the site contains graphic pornographic images. They are then given the opportunity to leave the site

Some sites require payment to view the contents and have an interactive section where the viewer can enter credit card information. This is a system that assumes persons under the age of 18 do not have a credit card and could not have access to someone else's card. That should not be a guaranteed assumption. I know of a friend's dog got a credit card.

The bottom line is simple: Children and adolescents with Internet access can easily access graphic pornographic sites. The less they are monitored by parents, the more apt they are to visit such sites.

Pornography is not perhaps the worst content a child can access on the Internet. Sites that promote racial violence, hate crimes, and other intolerable behavior are readily accessible. I know a young man who lived in a small town in Northern Washington who was smarter than his 15 years belied. He found a recipe for napalm on the Internet, and tried small amounts on rocks at the beach. This grew tiresome quickly and he calculated what he would need to destroy a crane at a local construction site. He succeeded, and paid for this crime for years.

I use this story as an example of other types of inappropriate information a child can find on the Internet. The push back I get is this information is available in books in the library, as is the recipe for meth amphetamines. My response is simple; a teenager is more apt to download the recipe for napalm in the privacy of his or her bedroom than copy it from a book in the library where he or she might be seen by others.

Here is where we face the American dilemma. If we lived in a brutal dictatorship that suppressed free speech, this subject would not be a chapter in this book. However, we enjoy the freedom of speech and the library and Internet service providers are loath to control the content accessed through their systems. The balance is to create an environment that fosters the freedom of speech and still recognizes that children progress in their intellectual development and certain content is inappropriate. Given there are laws that basically cover exposure to pornography, it is up to the parent to determine if the child can then access any and all other content.

EXPLOITATION

As mentioned previously, *MSNNBC* has run several episodes of *To Catch a Predator* where adults appear in chat rooms as children or adolescents. Adults enter the chat room and find these "children" and proceed to tempt them into a sexual tryst. Decoys that look like 13-year-old boys and girls are waiting in what seems to be an empty upper-middle class house. The adult enters, thinking he has made some significant progress toward having sex with a minor. Chris Hansen then appears and confronts the adult, who stutters through some flimsy excuse or explanation and leaves in a hail of shame only to be arrested by the local authorities.

There is some scandal over the general ethics of the operations of this program, but local police officials are thankful for the help in identifying real threats to childhood safety in their jurisdictions. Some of these perpetrators plead out their cases while others are determined to fight a good defense. Regardless, television has found a way to identify the modus operandi of child sexual predators, Internet chat rooms.

The danger of exploitation for families is when the computer is used without supervision. A family night out with a movie and a cheap dinner is better than a child trying to meet people in a chat room. Sports, chess club, dancing lessons, or even study groups at the library are a better alternative. I suggested this to some young parents who lived through the ever-more intellectual '90s and they said flat-out that they agreed. They controlled access to the Internet and were proactive about spending free time with their adolescent children.

INTERNET ADDICTION

Mental health professionals did not take long to discover people can become addicted to the Internet. While this chapter references the vulnerability of children and adolescents, much of what is written here is consistent with the findings of studies on adult addiction to the Internet.

Many child and adolescent therapists have told me they do not believe Internet addiction is an addiction per se, but rather another anomaly they have not precisely defined. As an author primarily of technical books, I felt the need to call on a nationally recognized specialist on Internet addiction. I was referred to Dr. Kimberly Young of The Center for Internet Addiction Recovery to guide me through some of the basic issues pertaining to Internet addiction especially among children and adolescents.

Dr. Young defines Internet addiction as exhibiting signs of "being preoccupied with the Internet, using it longer than intended, lying or concealing the nature of online use, withdrawal when forced to go without it, disobedience at time limits, and continued use despite consequences such as failure in school or broken relationships with others." She recommends the *Parent Child Internet Addiction* for identifying the most common symptoms of Internet addiction.

Dr. Young said that there has been no substantial research done to show that any particular age bracket or group is more susceptible to the addiction than another, but her belief is that males and females are just as likely to become addicted to the Internet, males more with gaming, gambling, and pornography and females more on chat systems or social sites. Her recommended strategy for preventing addiction would be to control where the computer is placed in the home, consider eliminating Internet access in computers in children's bedrooms, and to monitor children's Internet activity.

"Parents need to stay involved, learn how much time their children spend online, who they are talking with, and most important, get them involved in offline activities such as clubs at school or hanging out with family and friends. The computer should not be used as an electronic babysitter and with double income families it means that children are left alone for long periods of time. Careful monitoring and constant involvement in a child's life will reduce the potential risk of addictive or inappropriate use. It is also the same prevention for Internet predators— knowing who your children IM or MYSPACE with almost a necessity for parents today," Young advised.

If you suspect your child may have an internet addiction, Young suggests contacting a school counselor, child psychologist, your state or the national psychological association, which can be accessed from www.netaddiction.com.

Chapter 22: Exploitation of the Elderly

It would be easy to think that only children are at risk on the Internet, but people of all ages are victims of Internet predators. This section will examine specific threats to the elderly. The victimization is unique perhaps to the age group, but no less abusive. There are three prevalent categories of threats: exposure to malicious code; monetary exploitation; and identity theft.

EXPOSURE TO MALICIOUS CODE

I recently joined the American Association of Retired Persons (AARP), though I am quite a few years away from actually retiring. As I searched for deals I can get with my freshly printed AARP card, I chanced on some forums and chat rooms devoted to travel, some of them focused on making travel for the elderly cheap and interesting. These sites are in no way officially associated with AARP, but I found my way there as I tried to link up with other members. Once my email address was known to the members (it was required as my log in to the site) I began to get several unsolicited travel offers. This innocent spam might ordinarily be welcome—some of the deals were pretty good—but as I opened some of them, my virus and spybot alerts went off. These were isolated and deleted by my protective software, but anyone who was genuinely trying to find affordable travel and did not have protective software would immediately be infected.

The sad part about this incident was the truly innocent nature of the search: travel information and deals. Whoever hosted the site or hijacked the email addresses was intending to victimize a specific target, the elderly. Their site was designed in such a manner as to invite people to visit the site with the hopes of finding a fun, affordable vacation and in return, they were being infected with spybots.

Downloading and installing protective software to ward off these threats is often confusing especially for people who have not grown up in the technological age and lived their daily lives with computers. This issue will diminish as the generations who have lived with computers continue to age. However, the generation that preceded the introduction of cheap personal computers and access to the Internet desires to use the Internet for all of the same reasons anyone else does. I have spent some time volunteering at senior centers training members on how to secure their computers and on safety tips when using the Internet, but there are many people who do not have access to this training.

I have long advocated that vendors collaborate on developing Internet-ready computers for the elderly that are preconfigured for security. This market segment is not large. Security software companies will make their money from a different segment, and this can be seen as an opportunity to give back to the community for public relations.

Short of getting secure computers out of the box, there is a need to educate and assist the elderly who want to use the Internet. More often, these users are alone at home and may not be savvy to the symptoms of an infected computer. Once they are aware of it, they also may not want to admit the mistake and ask for help. That fear is not the province of the elderly; I work with several people who act that way every day. However, as we encourage the elderly to use the Internet, we need to proactively educate and assist them in protecting their computers.

MONETARY EXPLOITATION

My parents were raised in a generation that knew suffering and self-sacrifice during the Great Depression and then World War II. Survival often meant sharing and bartering with others. Out of that experience, many times I saw my father, a very fine carpenter, ply his craft without pay but in exchange of services, especially from our family attorney. I also saw my parents donate regularly and generously to their church. They had a finely tuned sense of generosity toward other people that was tempered by their standards for being truly needy. They didn't give much to people who were just lazy and conniving, but they did help people who were truly needy.

I see a different approach to this in my siblings and then my nieces and nephews. My generation is not as trusting and we tend to be more caustic toward those who do not take care of themselves. I am not sure which approach is truly better, but I can say with confidence it is the generosity of my parent's generation that puts them at risk for financial exploitation. Gen X, Y and now even Z users do not see computers as becoming ubiquitous, but as much a part of their daily lives as lunch, and maybe even more so. Most of them have never known a time when there were no computers. They have used computers for almost every social interaction, school work, entertainment and purchasing and have learned not to trust certain sites or individuals.

One of the most common attempts to steal comes in the form of an email. The recipient is treated to a sad story (and there are numerous versions of this sad story) of a wealthy official in a foreign country who needs to transfer his life savings and would like the kind assistance of someone who would cash a large cashier's check, keep a substantial portion of the money, and deposit the rest in a designated foreign account. Of course, the cashier's check is bogus, but this is not discovered until after the deposit is made into the foreign account and the person who cashed the check is liable for the full amount. My generation would immediately scoff at such a proposal and delete the email. However, too many elderly people have been caught in the scam and have lost substantial amounts of money simply for making the mistake of actually trusting someone.

My mother is targeted by charities asking for donations based on her address. Her home is located in a fairly affluent neighborhood and the phone banks hired to canvass for these donations call during the middle of the day. The assumption is they will probably get a retired person with some money and they can try to squeeze a donation out of him or her.

This same tactic is used through email. I received just such a solicitation in an email from a bogus charity that mentioned my participation in an online investment forum.

It was assumed that if I regularly visit the forum and exchange information about investing, I probably have money. I wrote a brief blog about this type of pernicious scamming over a year ago and got a lot of hot response from potential and actual victims, most of them retired and spending part of their golden years researching methods for maximizing their retirement savings. They naively figured their activities in the forum or other areas where investment information was exchanged would not be a target of scams, but where a con artist smells money he sets up shop.

As noted earlier, a tactic that I now employ quite aggressively is never to give out personal information when joining a new information-based forum or a recreation based social site. In spite of the best intended promises to keep my information private, I know better. I created a free junk email account that I would never use for my actual email correspondence for the purpose of having a legitimate email when a site requires it, and I check it once in a while. I log in, scan a few of the email titles and just delete everything. No one I would want an email from would ever be given that address. I don't like the notion of living in the shadows, but on the Internet I have realized this is pretty good advice.

IDENTITY THEFT

The issue of identity theft will be covered in more depth later in this book, but for the purposes in this chapter, there are a few special considerations regarding the elderly. After spending many tough years during the Depression and World War II, my parents became part of a huge middle class. One of the prerequisites for staying in the middle class and retiring comfortably was having good credit. People like my mother who no longer really need a line of credit have been well trained to pay bills on time and spend within their means. Their credit rating is gold.

Stealing the identity of a person with really great credit is a phenomenon that has grown almost out of control in the past decade. The elderly, in particular, are a target for this kind of scam.

I check several websites on security and I am particularly interested in case studies of methods for preventing Internet fraud perpetrated against the elderly. Time and again, I read about incidents involving in home care, relatives, and other trusted individuals who have access to the required information and succeed in stealing the identities of the elderly. This kind of an event usually comes to an awful end when an elderly person gets a bill for thousands of dollars in unpaid credit card debt.

This kind of proximity is not the only way for the elderly to be victimized. One email I saw floating around the Internet last year declared the recipient the winner of a special Microsoft giveaway. It had absolutely nothing to do with Microsoft but the website owner illegally used the Microsoft logo and called it a customer appreciation award. Too many people, many of them needy elderly, supplied their personal data including social security numbers and bank account numbers and then suffered drastic losses of money as a result as well as abuse of their financial identity.

As a part of my research, I went to the Social Security website and looked at how I could obtain information about my own account. I could request the information online, but it required so much personal information that there was an advisory at the top of each form cautioning me to make sure no one could see the screen and to not print out the form before I submitted it.

I regularly scan for key-loggers on my computers. This is a form of spybot that allows the person who placed it on your computer to record everything you type into your computer. In spite of assurances from many public access computer owners, such as the public library, of tight security measures, I know several administrators of such computer labs who do not have any kind of budget for sophisticated scanning software applications that would find a key-logger.

The best advice would be to avoid conducting any financial business that might require a comprehensive list of personal data on the Internet unless you are sure of the security of your system. Even if a website assures you their site is secure, your computer may not be.

The term *pharming* describes a practice where website owners replicate the look of sites such as Microsoft or eBay and redirect users to the site where they ask for personal information. Users think they are really on the eBay site when in reality they have been redirected. Be assured, sites such as eBay or your bank do not ask for personal information other than your log in or user name and encrypted password. You can probably guess the site is not legitimate if it looks like a trusted website but is seeking very personal information before you can enter.

CONCLUSION

As I spoke with individuals involved in information security about these three issues and the abuse of the elderly over the Internet, they cautioned that I not consider these victims as ignorant or unskilled. Quite the contrary, I concur they are, so far, our greatest generation who brought this country out of depression and through the Second World War. These guys aren't slouches. However, the success perpetrators have had victimizing this population I think stems from their inherent trusting nature. My generation is far more cynical, but no less a victim because of it, as we will explore in the next chapter.

Chapter 23: Viruses, Rootkits, and Spyware; The Evil Trio

Conventional computer wisdom for so many years warned strictly against viruses attached to emails and there was relatively little emphasis placed on more pernicious forms of attacks on personal and company-owned data and assets.

When I taught programming, I wanted the students to understand that a program can be written to do just about anything we want. In an introductory class, I posed a question and a project for extra credit: Write a program that will search for personal data in a standard Windows directory structure. Of course, they succeeded, some more than others. In a more advanced programming class, these same students were offered another extra credit project: Write a program that can piggyback an email attachment undetected and locate itself in a file or directory where it can monitor and log all Internet activity on a given computer and occasionally send this log file to a specific port on another computer. This is more difficult than the first assignment, but three students were amazingly successful.

While this might be perceived as intrusive behavior, there are legitimate applications for such a program. A parent might want a legitimately licensed program that reports all Internet activity on all computers at home on a regular basis. As a network administrator, I used similar log files regularly to monitor employee Internet access.

In the wrong hands, however, this type of program, known as a *spybot,* is a regular byproduct of a visit to websites that may or may not be related to the website content. Someone associated with the site sends the program to an open port and it functions as a monitor for illicit purposes. The spybot is not necessarily programmed to destroy data or diminish hardware functionality; its primary function is to collect specific types of data.

The viruses of the late '90s were brute force attacks on data and infrastructure. Downloading patches and antivirus updates did a fairly good job of offering protection from this type of malicious attack. However, with the rise in identity theft, corporate spying, and data mining, the plan of attack has changed dramatically. Instead of destroying the data, it is more valuable to steal or copy the data over long periods of time.

Early on, cookies placed on a computer were seen as necessary to speed up the return to any given website, especially a site where the user has decided to allow the site to remember his or her log in user name and password. Many virtual communities and information-based sites want to personalize your experience of their site so they ask you to create a membership profile. To reduce the number of passwords you need to memorize, these sites offer to place a cookie on your computer that holds your log in information and password. When you launch the site, a program running on the site searches for the cookie and reads the log in and password and places them in the proper dialogue box. In a few seconds you are logged in.

Imagine the power of such a program in the wrong hands. A very good programmer can use this same framework for a program that is not voluntarily downloaded and that reads every keystroke on your computer and logs them in plain text. Don't stop there. Why not a program that would identify banking, tax, legal, and investment accounts and copy this material to a log that is accessible to someone at a website you visit regularly?

Quietly, banks, schools, and government agencies are dealing with this issue. The primary source of this type of attack is not necessarily external, and in fact, the majority of these come from inside the network. One financial aid administrator for a private school hired an individual with extensive experience with federal financial aid programs. The person was really on a secret payroll of a competing school and was allowed to hire out to work the temp job offered. During his tenure, he placed five or more spybots on other financial aid workstations and the competing school was able to track certain types of data transactions, which revealed real numbers for enrollment, percentages of self-pay versus financial-aid students, and other useful data. Fortunately, the network administrator conducted regular audits of installed applications and discovered the programs.

Steps and strategies for preventing and combating viruses, rootkits, and spyware are discussed in chapter 31.

Chapter 24: The Phenomenon of Craigslist

Early in the 1980s, the use of a home computer was not something the vast majority of people would have considered. I recall one of my first home computers, A Commodore 64, was sitting on a table next to my small television. A friend visited to watch a movie (then played on a VCR) and wanted to know what kind of television would have a keyboard attached to it. I tried to demonstrate what the potential of this contraption would be by demonstrating a program I had written. He shook his head and saw no use for such a piece of garbage.

To find and communicate with other people who bought and used computers at home, bulletin board services (BBS) was formed, where information from programming tips to social news about clubs and restaurants could be exchanged.

In 1995, or so it is stated on their website, a man with the first name Craig established Craigslist, essentially a vastly improved version of the old BBS services. This community bulletin board took off, however, and today, every major city in the world has a Craigslist page listing everything from volunteer opportunities, groups for running, reading, and yoga to reading the bible. Early on it was recognized that technical talent could be more easily recruited through such a site and now many companies post jobs, no matter what managerial level, on Craigslist first.

The phenomenon of Craigslist is now legendary, but even the people behind this site acknowledge there are risks to completing business or personal transactions over the

Internet. When you visit the site, you will immediately notice there are sites for every major city and even smaller cities in remote areas. The principle of doing business only with local people is good advice even when using the Internet. The people at Craigslist place this advice prominently in their section on scams and risks. If you want a cheap fireplace insert, you will probably find one in your city, town, or neighborhood through Craigslist. There is no need to risk being scammed by sending money to someone half way across the country and never receiving the item.

Craigslist has become a substitute for the local newspaper want ads. People can buy anything from cars to land and at the same time set up a date for Friday night. The popularity of this simple to use and extensive list of local information has grown phenomenally.

My own experience with the list was been mostly positive with some mixed results. For example, I moved from Seattle to Southern California in February of 2007. I had decided to hold a garage sale. In the past, this meant picking a weekend date, calling the newspaper on Tuesday, advertising on Thursday, Friday, and Saturday at some considerable expense, and hoping people would read the listing. I also tried placing 3×5 cards on grocery store bulletin boards with little success. I placed a posting on Craigslist the morning of the sale at 7:30 AM, intending to be ready for the sale by 10:00, and posted that time. By 9:00, however, my driveway was full and people were buying things as I brought them out to the carport. Everything I had intended to sell was gone before noon. I continued to pack and clean throughout the day and late arrivals complained they had the same experience with every garage sale they saw on Craigslist; the stuff was gone before lunch time.

My next interesting experience was when I was ready to load the truck and I had 10 to 15 items I just wanted to give away. I posted on craigslist at 7:00 AM, and by 7:10, as I was getting ready to place the items in the yard, four trucks were waiting for me and the items never touched the ground.

As an associate dean, I was tasked with recruiting underpaid adjunct faculty. The kind of talent I needed was very specific and the normal method of advertising in the newspaper produced almost no results. At the beginning of my tenure in 2000, I regularly posted a notice on Craigslist and also scoured the resume section. In seven years, I was never without a qualified instructor who was ready and willing to teach their specific technical skill. The only set back I experienced was finding a resume for a man who claimed to be holding the job I held, at the very same campus. I called him and he persisted with the lie even when I explained that I was the associate dean of the campus.

So again, for every positive and great thing we find on the Internet there is also a potentially negative counterpart. The Internet is a double-edged sword.

Case in point, I attempted to sell a 1989 Isuzu Trooper on Craigslist. I got three different responses to the posting that insisted I sell the vehicle to them even though they were not in Seattle. I got explicit instructions about taking a certified check, cashing it, and paying to have the vehicle shipped to another state. While I liked the Trooper and would buy another one, I didn't think anyone would go to such extremes to acquire one that needed transmission work.

Craigslist provides a link on their pages titled "Avoid Scams and Fraud" and it is apparent they are very aware of this type of scam—and many other types of potential scams—including a variation on the scam I noted in chapter 7 about the wealthy finance minister from some unknown country needing us to cash certified checks and the scam that revolves around lottery winning notifications.

I have posted my resume on Craigslist with mixed success, but that may be mostly due to my misspelled words. I read the Craigslist warnings many years ago, and began to receive the exact types of scam offers they note, specifically an immediate job offer to accept wire transfers into my bank account and then to transfer most of the money on to another account, keeping a substantial portion of the funds. I would think someone would see this for what it is without the Craigslist warning; money laundering and somewhere along the line I would expect to either be ripped off or go to jail, if not both.

If I am selling or buying over Craigslist, I want to establish contact with the person so I might be able to verify who they are or track where they go after the transaction. I always ask for a phone number, a full name, and if possible, an address where I can pick up or deliver the goods. If they stall in giving me any of these, I am guessing the deal is too good to be true.

I try to stay away from urban legends that have no real basis in fact, but I listen to stories about people who actually believed the amazing offers and got involved in the transaction, only to lose their retirement savings. I have yet to meet anyone who has actually suffered this, but I am sure there are enough to cause official concern.

Finally, after moving to Southern California, I noticed a newspaper article about a young woman from a local University who had requested a ride on an Internet-based community bulletin board. She disappeared and, at the time of publication, has not yet been found. The article I read did not name Craigslist and there may be no connection. Nevertheless, there are many bulletin boards where people can exchange information about needing a ride or offering their vehicle to transport someone.

I placed a notice on a different bulletin board specifically designed for exchanging rides. I was offering to give someone a ride down the West Coast. I got two responses; neither individual wanted a ride they just wanted me to transport "sealed boxes" to somewhere in Los Angeles. I deleted my posting and closed my account on that site.

There are numerous bulletin boards and social networking sites that allow individuals to meet with the idea of dating and perhaps forming a relationship. Every responsible board or social site will list the potential risks of online dating. The most innocent of these risks is the lying about age and income. Then there are the lies about physical appearances and condition and also attributes. It slides downhill fast from there. Some people will post only to make a causal, sexual contact and while that is not illegal between consenting adults, there is huge risk to allowing a minor to pose as an adult only to be caught in a situation he or she is not ready to handle. In my closing comments in this book, I have some suggestions for managers of social sites and bulletin boards that may help reduce this risk.

Bulletin boards such as Craigslist offer very valuable information about the local community. While the vast majority of people will use it for nothing more than selling old skis and trading baseball cards, if you intend to use these types of bulletin boards, be sure to educate yourself on the information these sites offer regarding scams and risks they are aware of. Their intent is to help ensure your experience with their site is safe and rewarding.

Chapter 25: Getting the Wrong Message; The Problem with Wikis

A young journalist several years ago invented more than two dozen stories for a well-established and respected magazine. The journalist was fired for his total lack of ethics. In spite of our skepticism of what many consider a slanted news media, obvious and blatant falsification of information for mainstream media is still considered a firing offense.

In a few instances, this same standard of journalistic ethics is maintained on the Internet, but in just a few instances. If a website is associated with a mainstream news source, the standards for vetting and verifying information prior to publication are normally met. There are always going to be exceptions, but for the most part, if the information is not entirely accurate, an attempt has been made to validate it.

There are websites that knowingly offer false information that is salacious and even verges on libel or that write and publish false information with the intent of harming someone's character. Long ago, I gave up trying to get even the most basic news from Internet forums. I go to the Internet for entertainment, not necessarily the truth.

That is a very harsh statement, but one I stand behind. Too many so-called news sources or online commentary forums are based on prejudice, opinion, and unsubstantiated lies. For entertainment purposes only, I tracked a long line of interconnected sites devoted to a few common conspiracies. One site went so far as to claim that the head of a Catholic Religious Order stationed in Rome is actually the ruler of the world. For appearances, one or two former members of the order were quoted because they had "inside information." I got a good laugh out of it, as I do with most sites devoted to conspiracies that offer no substantial proof of their claims.

During most of the past major national and state election seasons, I turn to the politically based websites for entertainment, not information about one candidate or another. Any second-year college student who takes a course in rhetoric and debate knows the rules; if you make a claim, prove the claim with evidence, not pure speculation and prejudice.

While the bantering between politicians can be seen as a fun diversion, the real risks of being exposed to false information get serious when it comes to medical, financial and legal advice. A quick search resulted in an index of over 200,000 websites devoted to uncovering or identifying false medical information on the Internet. The scope and content of the sites covered medical issues ranging from the treatment of cancer to AIDS. There were sites devoted to identifying charlatans and quack medical devices. Rather than waiting for the snake oil salesman to come through town with his wagon, all we need to do is look up an illness on the Internet and find a plethora of unconventional and even harmful potential cures. Moreover, if you start checking what may be very benign symptoms that you are experiencing, you will quickly become convinced you have you have some grave or very rare condition that the Internet will provide along with the advice to contact your medical professional immediately.

This same problem exists among Internet-based financial advice. Web developers motivated by the objective of promoting sales can create any number of misleading information, charts, customer claims, and other information that can be totally false. Many stockbrokers and financial advisers have been doing this over the phone for years, and they are often—but not always—caught. The Internet is just a larger canvas for the same old practice.

Trying to determine if the information on a particular website is accurate and truthful can be a difficult task. The best method is the age-old practice in medicine of getting another opinion. This holds true for any kind of crucial information: medical, financial, political, or even theological. Do not trust one isolated source of information. Cross-reference the topic through a search engine and determine the sources. Often the source is more important than the actual information.

Taking this concept of misleading information into the personal arena, we need to examine the ever-increasing examples of two types of false information. First, companies are able to alter information on wiki sites where the data is dynamic and can be changed by almost anyone with Internet access. For example, let's say an oil company crashes a tanker into the rocks off the Canadian shore. Canadians add eyewitness information to the wiki site about how far off course the tanker was. The oil company executives can easily remove or alter those eyewitness accounts to serve their public relations goals. Ultimately, these kinds of sites, then, may not contain accurate information.

Secondly, a friend of mine started a website where he would personally serve notice to someone that you wanted to end a friendship. The intention was not mean spirited, and I thought it was a humorous creation. Some people, however, took the intent of the site too literally and upon receiving a notice to end a friendship, instead of contacting the person about the joke, they proceeded to post false and damaging information about that person on topic-related forums. I also know of a scorned boyfriend who posted mean and spiteful information about his ex-girlfriend on social sites she frequented with the clear idea of damaging her reputation. At some point, this kind of activity becomes libelous.

The issue of libel on the Internet is fairly new and just now being addressed through the courts. There are two issues that make this problem complex. First, it is easy to conceal your real identity on many forum sites where this type of information can be posted. It is often difficult to determine exactly who posted the information. It can be done by tracing the source computer if the forum site is logging that type of information. After identifying the computer, it would then be necessary to determine who was sitting at the computer at the time the message was posted. The second difficulty, once it is ascertained that the originator of the posting cannot be determined, is determining whether the website owner had knowledge of the offending information and did nothing about it. People who are victims of Internet libel can scroll to the bottom of any website and contact the webmaster. This may or may not be the website owner, but it is the person of legal record for people to contact about the site. Victims can explain

186

that the information is false and request it be removed. The webmaster may choose not to comply with the request, and legal action must be initiated by the victim. (Do not confuse this action with what is known as a "Take Down Notice," a legal process available to those who believe their copyrights have been infringed upon.) In the end, action can be taken against the website owner.

It is always best to first consult an attorney before taking any action regarding libel on the Internet. In fact, it is advisable to contact an attorney before attempting any kind of online or back-channel response.

PLAGIARISM

One final consideration of false information on the Internet focuses on students. As a college professor, I warned students both about plagiarizing material and also about accessing only one or two sites when researching a topic for a paper.

The plagiarizing issue is of concern to any academic. My own work from a security blog I write has ended up in student papers with no attributions to me as the author. The student just cut and pasted my paragraphs into his or her own paper. This activity is usually easy to detect; writing styles differ greatly and even subtle differences between paragraphs can be detectable. Most academics are very adept at this. It is also easy to type one or two sentences into a search engine if the material is suspected of being plagiarized. I could usually find the original source of the stolen material and the website the student stole it from in less than five minutes, and then attach it to the student's paper with an 'F' on the top.

The subject of using inaccurate information in an academic paper is of greater concern. I have always advised students to avoid using any wiki site that can be altered by the users for academic research. These sites have too often been the source of completely inaccurate information. Students should know how to search for peer-reviewed articles and books on any given topic. These courses have been read and challenged by other academics with the same or similar specialty. Hopefully, the author took the challenges seriously and revisited his or her research before producing the material.

The old saying about believing half of what you see, a quarter of what you read, and nothing of what you hear is good advice when it comes to information on the Internet. It is far too easy to post false or inaccurate information on a website. Cross reference anything you need to take seriously and find sources other than the Internet in this process.

Chapter 26: Who Would Want to Be Me?
The Truth about Identity Theft

The Department of Justice (DoJ) claims identity theft is one of the fastest growing crimes in the world It is clear from the publicity around this type of crime, that identity theft is not limited to just the illegal use of a credit card.

A passport from a so-called first-world country is valuable to persons aspiring to enter one of those countries without being properly identified. Theft of U.S. passports has long been the focus of drug smugglers, money launderers, and more recently terrorists. Either the thieves change the photograph in the passport or find someone who very closely resembles the actual person who was originally issued the passport.

Identity theft is a complex issue and requires some specific expertise in order to shape the most effective policies to prevent it and the most effective response in the event it happens. Robert Siciliano, CEO of IDTheftSecurity.com, who specializes in identity theft, agreed to be interviewed on this topic for this book.

The interview began with a pretty standard question: Once a person has personal identifying information, such as full name, mother's maiden name, social security number, birth date, and address, other than opening a credit card account using my name, what could they do with it? Siciliano suggested the person who has obtained this kind of information can go on to can get a driver's license under your name, open up any kind of account you can open, get a job, go to school, get married, have kids, and do anything you can do using your name, posing as you.

I asked him whether there is an actual crime committed if someone does open an account using my information. Siciliano replied that the Identity Theft and Assumption Deterrence Act makes assuming anyone's identity a crime. Other than that, depending on the types of fraud someone commits, he or she is more than likely to commit wire fraud and/or racketeering, and is more prone to break other laws.

Earlier in this book, I warned readers about the technology known as key logging, where an application is running that records and archives and then even sends remotely every keystroke entered into a computer. When asked if Siciliano sees a rise in the use of this in reference to identity theft, he stated that key-logging is the technology that made hackers change their motivation from seeking fame to now seeking fortune. A key-logger can be installed in any PC whether a hardware or software key-logger that records everything you do on your PC or a public terminal. He added this is a favorite tactic used by certain terrorist cells and others who want to move or create illicit, illegal, or incriminating data.

Once the crime of identity theft is committed and a perpetrator succeeds at securing a credit card, it seems obvious these people are then able to perpetrate more crimes using that credit card. Siciliano agreed with this assessment stating one of the most—and most costly— common crimes is medical insurance fraud. He has also seen illegal residents having babies under assumed names, allowing their children to claim citizenship in the United

States. Using a driver's license with another person's name on it could easily result in a criminal record such as drunk driving, and from there the list goes on and on.

The focus of the interview shifted to prevention. I asked Siciliano if he recommended using credit cards for Internet purchases and he replied that he had no problem using credit cards online, over the phone, and so on. He claims you can't protect credit card numbers, and it's okay to use them. He noted that our responsibilities lie in carefully reviewing statements at the end of each billing cycle and refuting unauthorized charges within 60 days of potential fraud.

People live hectic lives and make mistakes. We know what life can be like especially if the house is full of kids. I wondered what mistakes people might make when they are rushing to get something done on the Internet that leaves them exposed. Siciliano agrees with the premise of much of this book, stating, "The biggest problems people face in their own homes is leaving user names and passwords written down on yellow sticky notes on the sides of monitors. Additionally, P2P software installed on a family PC can open up the entire family's personal information to identity thieves all over the world."

Siciliano suggests that the best practice or method to help home users from accidentally giving out personally identifying information is to secure computers with virus definitions, security patches, and remove spyware, and to "Never, never give out personal information over the phone to anyone who calls you. More than likely it's a scam. And never plug in any information in an email you receive requesting to update an account nor verify information."

I wondered how I can be certain the database an online retailer keeps with my personal data is secure. I know if I ask them they will nod their heads and say, "Yeah, sure it's safe," but is there a way of really finding out? Siciliano indicated there is no way to verify if a retailer is safe. Chances are it can be compromised one way or another. This is a fact of life. Regardless, as long as you check your statements and monitor your credit reports then you can mitigate any breaches that occur.

If data maintained by a school, for example, is compromised, school administrators are required by law to contact every person whose data was compromised and inform them of the event. This happened in the spring of 2010 at the University of Maine when the databases holding data about students who visited the campus counseling center. There were a number of reasons the data was vulnerable, but the immediate task of the administrators was to contact all of those students and inform them of the breach. The University of Maine also provided credit monitoring services for a year following the incident free of charge to all whose data had been compromised.

I posed two further questions to Siciliano. Once a commercial or retail database is compromised, are there laws requiring the owners of those databases to contact its customers and let them know of the compromise, and if there are no laws, how do consumers know if this has happened? He replied that most states have database breach notification laws in affect. "However," he warned, "don't wait for breaches to protect yourself. Consider your information already breached."

This response made me wonder what essential steps I must take immediately if I discover someone has illegally used my personal identifying information.

Siciliano quickly responded, "Check your credit, get a credit freeze, shred everything, and monitor your accounts closely. If this happens and your credit card is used, your liability for credit cards may be 50 dollars. However, the losses of time and money add up when your identity has been severely compromised. The costs can include lost time from work, attorney's fees, and sometimes hiring a private investigator."

Unfortunately, Siciliano doesn't believe any new technologies are imminent that will mitigate the threat of identity theft. "We aren't going to turn the corner for at least ten years," he said. "This problem will not get better until the systems of identification become much more secure and we have all been properly identified. Beyond protecting yourself, I suggest investing in identity theft protection. There are many companies offering up credit monitoring and web monitoring. This is the best way to stay proactive. I'd recommend McAfee Identity Protection."

Robert Siciliano can be reached at www.IDTheftSecurity.com.

SECTION III
SURFING SAFELY

Chapter 27: The Internet, Children, and the Law
- 18 U.S.C. §§ 2256(1) and (8)

The Internet as we know it today became popular once the World Wide Web was created, and also once Internet service providers and telecommunications companies began to expand the available bandwidth. However, just as soon as these two technologies allowed greater numbers of people to access the Internet, the problem of exploiting children was immediately recognized. The laws presently on the books were written in the mid- to late-1990s and while there is a continuing debate over their effectiveness and the need to change or update them, the underlying concern remains the protection of children.

Three laws stand out as being the most definitive and comprehensive in their scope. The first is 18 U.S.C. §§ 2256(1) and (8), defining child pornography and the remedies for those who engage in the manufacture, distribution, and possession of it. If you conduct a simple Google search of "18 U.S.C. §§ 2256(1) and (8), you will most probably be brought to the Cornell University Law School website. The entire code is there for anyone to read. The language may be fairly graphic, but it is also very specific.

Law enforcement officials, while diligent and effective in their work, admit there is still a lot of work to do when it comes to controlling child pornography. These deviants find clever ways to mask their activities.

I attended a lecture on cybercrime being committed by terrorists. One trick the presenters discovered terrorists were employing was the use of a single email account where everyone in the cell had the user name and password. Instead of sending email, the members of the cell wrote drafts and attached documents to the drafts and never sent them. At that time, email services were not scanning drafts; instead they were focusing on what was being sent. They soon realized the drafts for individual accounts were more numerous than the actual mail sent, and individuals were logging on from several different locations at the same time. When they began to crack this misuse of a free email service for transferring terrorist information, they discovered the technique was learned from child pornographers.

Doubtless both terrorists and child pornographers will continue to find more clandestine ways of communicating without immediate recognition, but I am confident technologists in law enforcement are adept and capable of finding them.

Another law that has proven to be effective in many cases is the Title XIII Children's Online Privacy Protection. The full text of this law is available at http://www.ftc.gov/ogc/coppa1.htm.

The scope of this law is to protect the identity of children 13 and under who use the Internet. Quoting directly from the law found on the site:

a) ACTS PROHIBITED.—

(1) IN GENERAL.—It is unlawful for an operator of a website or online service directed to children, or any operator that

has actual knowledge that it is collecting personal information from a child, to collect personal information from a child in a manner that violates the regulations prescribed under subsection (b).

(2) DISCLOSURE TO PARENT PROTECTED.—Notwithstanding paragraph (1), neither an operator of such a website or online service nor the operator's agent shall be held to be liable under any Federal or State law for any disclosure made in good faith and following reasonable procedures in responding to a request for disclosure of personal information under subsection (b)(1)(B)(iii) to the parent of a child.

In short, a website cannot collect or display personal information about anyone 13 years of age or younger. This means that even if a child is looking at a website and wishes to identify his or herself, the website owner must assist in preventing that. Children enjoy some protection, then, from predators who might wish to find them at a physical location. This law also helps to keep persons who do not have custody of a child from using the Internet to find and abduct a child.

Nevertheless, the law is not perfect. My book *The Tiger Guide to Information Security* details an incident involving a day care that allowed custodial parents to use a secure website where they could peek in on the day care center and watch their children during the day. The site was cracked and a father with no custody rights was able to observe his child and figure out where the day care center was located. Fortunately, this vulnerability was discovered by the astute mother of another child and after complaining about this, users were subsequently required to authenticate using credentials provided to them by the school.

The law is also imperfect in that a child can go on to a website, lie about his or her age and there is little in the way of access control preventing this. It is possible for a minor child to appear as an adult and make inappropriate contact with another adult, as discussed earlier in the section on social sites.

It is helpful to research other laws that are specific to your city or state. The FBI offers an abundance of information on their website (www.fbi.gov) that will help parents not only make good choices when trying to allow their children to use the power of the Internet for academic and entertainment purposes, but also to protect them from predators and inappropriate material. Every major municipal or county police department also has information and links that parents will find helpful.

It is helpful to understand that the World Wide Web grew faster than the judicial system could respond, but they have caught up and in a big way. At first, they had to interpret existing laws against a new digital technology when it came to finding, validating, and preserving evidence. Having done this, for the most part, they are now facing challenges regarding jurisdictions and activity in different countries that do not provide the same level of protections for their citizens.

At the writing of this book, there is a debate over how to interpret some of these laws and whether the laws restrict freedom of speech. Get involved in this process to ensure it is easier to help protect you child when they want to use the Internet.

Chapter 28: Internet User Policies

Up to this point, we have discussed basic networking concepts and documented the existing network as it is. To ensure we have at least a baseline understanding of how to surf the Internet safely at home and at work, it is important to map the way to an end point. We need to know what we want to secure, how to secure it, and how this affects the actions of legitimate users. What we need is a well-planned, written security policy.

Usually, there are no security policies in place, especially in a home or small business network. I have discovered this even in large, complex enterprise environments. Security policies seem like a tedious chore until it is too late.

Policies in printed form do not necessarily prevent malicious attacks on a network; they need to be adopted and implemented and they need to address properly the security issues specific to each network. To understand the process of getting to a comprehensive corporate security policy fully, I recommend *The Tiger Guide to Information Security,* which thoroughly covers this topic.

An astute parent or network administrator will already have an opinion about how secure the network environment is. Now, the work of shaping a living document that will grow with the network and provide levels of safety begins. For the sake of secure and safe home Internet usage, when I begin the policy phase, I ask parents the following:

- *Have you discussed with your children what it means to be exposed to age-appropriate material?*
- *Do they know why you want them to avoid specific subject matter?*
- *Do your children have unlimited access to the Internet at any time?*
- *Do you actively participate in Internet research required by your schools with you children?*
- *Is the computer located in an area of the home where anyone can see what is on the screen?*
- *Have you listed specific types of websites that are off limits at certain ages?*
- *Is it clear to your children the types of access controls, monitoring, and restrictions you have configured for their Internet access?*
- *Have you researched various methods for monitoring and restricting access?*
- *Are the consequences for violating the home-user policies appropriate, clearly understood, and enforced?*

When it comes to a small business, my questions are a bit different:

- *Does the documentation reveal a carefully planned internal and external strategy for securing data and computing assets?*
- *Are there regular updates of virus protection and are the procedures for this clearly stated?*

- *Is there a clear policy regarding who can access certain files and are they properly implemented in the operating system?*
- *Is there a clear understanding of the possible environmental hazards in the area and have proper mitigation procedures been put in place to minimize the effects of them?*
- *How does a new employee get a log in and password and how is that password managed; could I easily gain access to restricted files by lifting another employees keyboard and seeing his or her password?*
- *Can anyone access the wireless system?*
- *As the company adds new employees and grows, is there a plan in place that scales the network and the security at the same time?*
- *What happens if an employee or member of the family steals movies or downloads patently offensive material; are procedures in place to handle this issue properly?*
- *Is there a regular procedure for taking highly sensitive data to secure storage?*
- *Who is the keeper of the administrative password and how widely is that password distributed?*
- *Is there a concerted effort to plan for the dismissal or voluntary departure of key IT personnel properly?*

At each new location, the answers to these questions are usually negative. Most organizations wing it until there is a problem. Without a clear policy, say, for viewing and downloading even legal pornography, attempts to discipline the child may be futile or attempts at firing the person from a company may fail. The result in a working environment may be a sexual harassment lawsuit from people who are offended by the activity and the inability of the organization to stop it.

Without a complete and thoroughly tested policy, the downloading of pornographic material is a very small problem when you consider what else could happen. Further, once a policy is in place, it must be monitored for compliance and subsequently enforced. I don't need to tell parents how difficult is often is to discipline their children. Attempting to discipline an employee with a policy that is not consistently monitored or enforced will probably fail and may result in a lawsuit being filed by the employee.

This chapter is intended to help you develop a written policy that will lead to safe and secure Internet usage. It addresses each issue as it pertains to first the home environment and then a working environment. These then are the four basic steps toward developing an effective security policy:

1. Review potential risks.
2. Address specific issues with specific policies.
3. Educate, advise, and then implement the policy.
4. Review and modify the policy on a regular basis.

REVIEW POTENTIAL RISKS AND THE BUSINESS NEEDS OF THE ORGANIZATION

Internet usage exposes different people to different risks. As noted previously, children have three basic vulnerabilities; exposure, exploitation, and addiction. Other users in the home may have the same vulnerabilities, but add to this list the threat of identity theft. In a company, the risks are data security and integrity, personal identifying information, inappropriate or offensive exposure, and illegal use of the Internet.

What is essential now is to place a value on everything that falls within these categories. A database of customer names might regularly yield a company $3 million in sales in any given year. Is that the face value of the database if it was destroyed or stolen? How much could you insure the database for? A new rack of blade servers in a data center with all distribution hardware intact might cost about $300,000. How quickly does this value depreciate once it is in place and what is its value one month, one year, and five years after implementation? A proprietary CRM application costs $400,000 to plan, write, and implement. If someone was able to penetrate the security and ruin this application rendering it worthless, what value does that have in replacement and loss of business?

You will need to know these values in order to decide on a cost-effective security plan. The owner of these assets needs to decide how secure to make the network based on the value of the assets being protected. When it comes to protecting children, the elderly, and all other family members, this calculation sounds cold, but is essentially the same as in a working environment.

The British government spends sizeable sums of money protecting the crown jewels. A neighbor we had when I was in high school spent absolutely no money protecting the pile of old tires he had in his back yard. Translating that across to a computer network, if you have a few games and your favorite Internet links on your computer and there are no children in your home, safety is not much of a worry. However, if you are holding the electronic versions of the Department of Defense's plans for futuristic weapons, you spend time and money on security and Internet safety.

I make this point because many security plans fail when a proper value assessment is not made of people and assets and the security is either cost prohibitive to protect valueless assets or extremely valuable assets are permanently lost because no security was implemented. Provide security commensurate with the value of the asset.

Effective home-usage policies take into consideration how each unique parent decides to raise his or her children. I would never define a general policy for home usage unless requested to do so within the parenting philosophy of an individual family. Within the working environment, however, there are some concerns that are consistent across the board and a more generic policy can be developed that responds directly to these issues.

ADDRESS SPECIFIC ISSUES WITH SPECIFIC POLICIES

We discussed previously the "How to Catch a Predator" shows *Dateline NBC* has aired. The activity of adults masquerading as children and entering chat rooms with illicit intentions becomes illegal when any adult on the chat site begins to have a conversation with a child that is intended to lead to sexual activity, even if the "child" is an adult. In spite of the numerous times this show is aired, adults in chat rooms still try to sexually exploit children, some even admit when caught that they have viewed the program with the outcome of arrests and conviction.

A director of a well-funded program sat red-faced as local police investigated the loss of a data base of donors. The donors might have continued to give to the program, but the issue was not so much the loss of the database but the revelation of the personal assets and value of the donors. Some of the information became public and an extortion attempt followed to suppress the remainder of the personal data. The director had purchased an expensive firebox in addition to upgrading the routers. Everyone sat comfortably behind a well-guarded firewall. Nevertheless, the data was stolen from the inside as the network administrator watched dutifully at the perimeter for intrusions.

In another case study, a company spent thousands of dollars on antivirus and operating systems updates but failed to analyze the physical security of their building properly and 15 computers, including the servers and the data farm, were carried effortlessly out the door. The antivirus applications might have been necessary, but they could also have been excessive. What was not considered was the potential loss from theft. Maybe an alarm system and higher-quality locks would have been a better first purchase followed later by the antivirus protection.

It is important to list all of the potential risks, and once they have been prioritized by personal importance or dollar value, address each in a manner consistent with their value. This might show up in the security policy as procedures for very basic antivirus updating and procedures for extensive monitoring of physical security. This might also manifest itself as a list of specific types of websites that cannot be visited and those considered safe.

In a home environment, children may be prohibited from visiting chat rooms alone until they have reached a certain age. The family may also determine that a type of site may be visited at a certain age only after a discussion about the subject matter and its potential impact on the child. In a working environment, there can be a blanket policy prohibiting access to any kind of pornographic, hate-inspired, or other destructive types of websites. There can also be policies prohibiting the use of Instant Messaging or ActiveX controls.

EDUCATE, ADVISE, AND THEN IMPLEMENT THE POLICY

Once all of the risks have been evaluated and a proper response formulated, the policy is not going to be effective until people understand why it was written, what it hopes to attain, and how it impacts their behavior and then becomes a mandatory part of their home life or terms of employment. In the work environment, you should consult a lawyer to get through this.

Basic child psychology tells us that children want firm direction with consequences appropriate to the age and action. Of course, how that is interpreted from home to home varies. Nevertheless, my experience consulting with families about creating Internet usage policies for the home has proven this time and again. When children are clear on what is allowed and what is not, as well as what the consequences are for not complying and when they know the consequences are real, there is less concern about inappropriate use of the Internet.

Most managers now know that if they do not have written policies that are mandatory, presented, and consented to in writing by the employee, they virtually have no policies. This is really the easy part, though. After an introduction period, employees are required to sign an acceptance form of the new policies, which gives an implementation date, and following that date, they must comply with the new policies. A good lawyer will make fast business of this part.

The difficulty in introducing security policies, even after they become mandatory, is getting people to follow them. It is always preferable to have buy-in to the policy and willing participation than to have to penalize someone. This requires education.

The families I have consulted with who enjoyed the most success in implementing a home-user policy also engaged in conversations about the risks of the Internet with their children. The children knew it was serious business.

In a working environment, the most troublesome security breakdown is the tendency people have to write passwords in a notebook or on a slip of paper and keep them within arms' length of the keyboard in a drawer, under the keyboard, or pinned to the cubicle wall. Worse yet, an employee calls in sick, calls a friend at work, and gives him all of her passwords to check her email. Even when there were specific policies in place and the employee agreed to the policy in writing, I have conducted physical audits of workstations only to find 80 to 90 percent of the employees violating this policy. Moreover, even when the CEO warned them of reprimand and that the passwords would be confiscated and changed, many employees still failed to comply with the policy.

In both home and commercial environments, the need to provide a clean, safe and comfortable working environment is paramount and this covers the viewing and downloading of material others would find immoral or outright offensive. A security policy should also cover this and the topic needs to be discussed during routine sexual harassment presentations as well as upon hire.

It is advisable to conduct comprehensive network security training during orientation. Cover all issues pertaining to employee activity and behavior that affect the network.

In the enforcement of security policies, there has to be an iron fist inside a velvet glove. Violations of the security policy affect operations and could diminish profits. Berating and humiliating someone for an accidental violation might serve to break down morale and future desire to observe policies and I have known cases where employees have turned on their companies and tried to wreak as much harm as they could on the network after being humiliated. There might be cause for immediate dismissal, but all of this from innocent slipups of password management to outright intentional destruction of data should be handled professionally and in compliance with local human resource laws.

It's not funny to think of the number of network administrators who have nicknames like Attila the Hun and worse. Security Policies can be very powerful and might best be kept out of the hands of the power hungry. The policies are intended to secure the environment, assets, and data, not to give administrators a thing to bludgeon employees with.

REVIEW AND MODIFY THE POLICY ON A REGULAR BASIS

As conditions change, so must the security policy. Children mature and are ready for different kinds of material. In a working environment, new operating systems, new divisions within the company, and any change necessary to accommodate growth are introduced and this changes the need for security and safety. A company might begin to allow employees the ability to surf the Net whereas they did not previously allow it. This elevates the need for constantly updating antiviral protection. An outsourced company may be retained to provide desktop backup for all workstations and this would change how employees and internal administrators would deal with desktop issues.

Respond to these changes appropriately with the same considerations that developed the initial policies.

TESTING INTERNET USAGE POLICIES

Consider how a family or company should test safety and security. Should you allow someone on the outside to try and attack your systems? Should you plant someone on the inside to roam the hallways and try to gather whatever data they can and see if there are internal leaks? Yes to both.

There are legitimate companies who do "white hat" testing of external security. There are fewer companies who have staff well trained enough to test the internal systems. This is new to the industry.

External penetration testing will require written permission by the ultimate owner of the system and the specifications will be very clear as to what the test is looking for. Most legitimate penetration tests stop at the open port and proceed no further. Their report will make clear what they found and what the vulnerabilities are. This kind of test should be typically completed without the knowledge of the network administrator. Advanced knowledge of the test would possibly allow them to examine their own configurations ahead of time and make some corrections. This might be the desired outcome, but it is always good to have a silent and objective analysis of the system security.

The internal tests are a little more difficult to plan and implement, but they should include some social engineering to determine if personnel are sharing passwords, an audit of attempts to access restricted drives or files, a physical audit of workstations to see if passwords are easily accessible, and an audit of workstations to determine whether Internet use is compliant with company policies. Consult with company attorneys before conducting this kind of internal audit. I always want to know first if the employees are aware that the owner of the company has declared, in advance, the possibility of an audit occurring and whether the employee(s) has acknowledged this in writing. Without prior notice, it is always difficult to proceed with further education or disciplinary action for violations of policy.

I have always warned owners that they might not like what they see during the security audit. Their most treasured employee or the relative they are helping out might turn out to be extremely careless in his or her practices, or worse, malicious in attempts to destroy or steal data.

A good test will reveal any possible weaknesses. More importantly, internal weaknesses might point to a need to conduct more education on the need for security and the policies that define them.

Once a family or corporate policy is developed, there might be automatic buy-in and compliance, but don't bank on it. Later, we will discuss the need for proactive monitoring of Internet usage against the adopted policies.

Chapter 29: I Saw Where You Went Last Night... Monitoring Internet Use

When I speak or write about the more general subject of information security, I devote a significant amount of time and space to the subject of network monitoring. Typically, attendees to my seminars or those who have not read my books and blogs immediately think that network monitoring is all about watching what people do on the Internet. They get some pleasure thinking this is the heart of a security policy.

Monitoring Internet usage is the heart of an Internet user's policy, but it is only a small part of a general network security policy. While I consider this activity very important in a book about Internet safety, I want to underscore that there are many other important issues when it comes to general network security.

That being said, the act of monitoring Internet usage is not a glamorous activity. While necessary, it soon becomes less interesting than scrubbing dishes. When I managed a fairly large group of senior and junior network administrators, part of our general security plan was regular and proactive monitoring of Internet usage. The newbies were always assigned to the task; not by me, but by the other network administrators who had done their time reading logs and looking at thumbnails of sites users had visited.

I had written very clear procedures for this task. My first caution to anyone who takes on this role is you may not like what you see and you also may definitely find something that is patently illegal. Part of the Internet usage policy should include a well thought-out procedure in the event something that is seemingly illegal is found. The most important consideration in this event is to ensure that the "evidence" is not tainted in any way. Any business wishing to take on the monitoring of Internet activity is strongly advised to seek the advice of an attorney and the local law enforcement agency they would have to call in the event of finding illegal activity. They will help you craft an effective policy.

The policy of monitoring this activity should include clear, easy steps taken by the person conducting the monitoring so the local law enforcement agency can take effective steps to investigate and, potentially, prosecute the activity. My policies required the person undertaking the monitoring to immediately notify the local law enforcement agency responsible for investigating illegal Internet activity. This is typically first the local police who will then make any decisions for escalating an investigation. My policy also required the person who found the material to stay with and secure the computer and not allow anyone else to touch it until the police arrived. There was always a clear understanding that the person who finds and reports the material may be investigated. Indeed, monitoring Internet traffic is a serious endeavor.

Once you get past determining if the material is illegal, you will find material that is offensive. I don't say you *may* find it, I say you *will* find it. This applies to users at home and at work. Some people are not easily offended and they start the task of monitoring with a cold eye. They soon want to relinquish the task. I find most humor now to be less humorous and more offensive. What got a laugh last year is tame compared to what people chuckle about this year, and it becomes increasingly tasteless, and it is all easily available on the Internet.

After a month or so, most junior network administrators I know would rather do the company or family laundry than monitor Internet traffic. This, however, pales in comparison to the task of confronting the individual who has knowingly downloaded content that is in violation of user policies. A savvy Internet user knows there are many ways to access materials anonymously, and many can even spoof the name attached to the material. Unless your Active Directory is configured so all Internet activity is tied directly to system authentication, thereby leaving an indelible stamp associated with the website visited, proving an individual is responsible for consciously visiting an offending site can be difficult.

This can be easier in a family where a limited number of people access a certain computer and especially now when most children may already own their own computers. There is little argument about who accessed the site. This assumes that only children will violate the agreed upon policy. More than one adult relationship has ended after prolonged arguments over accessing porn, endlessly playing violent online games, and generally using the Internet as an escape from a relationship.

There is a standard response regarding improper Internet activity. When I needed to confront someone, most had already learned to blame the "pop ups." It is true some websites, when visited, will automatically launch pop ups, or small windows typically used for advertising. Many times these advertisements are for adult-oriented websites. However, most experienced administrators know that a user will not receive numerous pop-ups of the same kind of content.

When I was a newly minted senior network administrator with no staff, I took on the monitoring task. As administrator, I logged all Internet activity associated with an authentication name. If you logged on to my system, I logged your Internet activity. I would review these logs and look only for the uniform resource locator, the website name. There was so much activity that I could only hope to catch people who had visited sites with obviously noncompliant names. I discovered the long list of sex-related websites associated with the name of an individual who had taken a leave of absence. These sites were being visited on a computer that was located in a corner where no one could see the monitor. I set a simple webcam in the room and watched who went to the computer. At about the same time three days in a row, an individual sat down to the computer, logged in, and spent most of a lunch break there. After the person left, I audited the authentication logs and did not find his name there, but rather the name of an individual who was on a leave of absence. When I confronted him in the presence of two senior managers, he admitted the other person had given him the log in and password for his account and that he had used them to access pornography.

Now that we have established just how unpleasant this task will become, let's examine some of the most effective methods. The most common home remedy for monitoring Internet traffic is to look at the history of the browser. This is very elementary and even those who only occasionally view material on the Internet know that they can delete this after every session. The next step, in a Windows environment, is to look at the Local Disk C:\Documents and Settings\ or in Windows Vista or newer, C:\Users\...You will see the names of people who have logged on to the system. Pick the person you are monitoring, open this folder, and look through Cookies, Favorites, and any other folder you like. The cookies will show you every site the person has visited, but you will see trends and patterns. Typically, this was all I ever needed to confront someone.

There are off-the-shelf applications that can monitor and log all Internet traffic, most of which are unseen by the user. A robust list of these products can be found at Monitortools.com. Most of the products are for monitoring general network traffic, but there is a section specifically for monitoring Internet traffic.

There is a product called Big Brother that is a key-logger that will capture and log every keystroke a person makes on a computer. This is a very powerful tool for monitoring, but unfortunately my introduction to it was after searching for spybots on my computer and discovering someone had downloaded it to my hard drive.

There are very affordable chat-monitoring applications available. One I like is Ming Chat Detector. While this product is somewhat limited in comparison to others, Ming is very affordable. I have used this during seminars for middle and high school students. I asked a friend in my chat list if he was willing to have a chat session monitored. Using an overhead projector, I showed on one computer that I was chatting with this friend. Another computer on the wireless network launched the chat monitor, and in spite of the fact it was not running the chat session, it visually recorded every word in the chat session on the other computer. I have helped parents successfully implement this type of monitoring tool for all types of chat.

There are other strategies I alluded to in the previous chapter on policies. In my list of questions, I asked where the computer is located. If the answer is in the child's room behind a closed door, there is not much hope of effectively monitoring compliance with a family Internet usage policy. It would be better if the computer was located near the kitchen or family room where anyone could pass by and see what is on the monitor. One family may think it is perfectly fine to allow a child to surf the Net in the privacy of his or her room, and I am not here to argue with them, however, if you are at all concerned with the type of material a child is accessing on the Internet, the location of the computer is the first step toward being in control of that activity.

One family I worked with ten years ago in Denver created a progressive schedule based on age and the conversation the parents had with the children as they grew up. They did not allow the children to access the Internet until they were at least 7 years old. Between 7 and 10, all Internet activity was conducted when one or both of the parents were actively present at the keyboard. Between the ages of 11 and 13, the parents located the computer in the kitchen and could walk by the monitor at any time. Between the ages of 14 and 16, the computer could be located in the teen's bedroom with the door open. Until the children reached the age of 16, the parents disconnected their computers from the Internet after 10:00 PM and reconnected them at 7:00 AM. Once the teens were beyond 16, their access was unrestricted. At every progressive stage, there were formal and informal discussions about the good and bad of the Internet, just as there were discussions about sports, the dangers of drugs, the importance of school work, and the like. The parents wove the reality of the Internet into their family life.

I have checked up with this family occasionally over the years and they have stuck to the program in spite of a few protest arguments. They report there is a balanced approach to Internet use, and it is primarily for academic purposes. As the teens approached college application age, there was very heavy use of the Internet researching colleges and preparing their applications. There was the occasional curiosity search for sexual content, but this was easily monitored and the proper consequences were applied.

No monitoring plan is perfect for the home or for the work place. There will be some level of noncompliance with any policy. As a senior network administrator, I instructed those tasked with monitoring to go and find the instances of noncompliance. They thought they should simply wait for it to happen and I told them it is happening and their job was to find it so we could apply some form of reprimand. It was important to our attorneys that there was a policy in place, traffic was being actively monitored for compliance and violators were evenly reprimanded.

Without those three elements, they were adamant we would never be able to enforce serious violations.

Monitoring Internet traffic is truly an unpleasant task. I am happy I am not responsible for that portion of the network, but I am also happy there is a strict policy and someone is doing that job.

Chapter 30: Don't Go There!
Restricting Internet Access

Before depending too much in restricting Internet access, consider the implications. There are methods for completely or selectively blocking access or for allowing access only to specific sites. The most decisive method is to disconnect the computer from any Internet connection, cancel the ISP account, and live without the Internet, period. When any of these methods are deployed, it is clear those in charge do not trust the users. If the consequences of this are acceptable, then use any or all of these methods at will.

In the previous chapter, I mentioned a family in Denver who routinely disconnected computers from the Internet at night. They had no problem with this practice. To them it was the same as leaving a cake out in the kitchen and then hoping their children would not be tempted to eat it. In spite of many conversations about eating healthy, they knew what would happen to the cake. Until they felt their children would make wise choices when surfing the Internet after hours, there was no Internet at night.

As a network administrator, I lived with a management policy that directed me to limit access to the Internet for individuals who had violated the Internet usage policy. Using a group policy object, I "quarantined" the individuals and allowed access only to sites sponsored by the company for conducting internal business. This same method can be used system wide. One company I'm aware of restricts external access and limits all Internet browsing to the Intranet sites the company uses for information and conducting business.

There are some simple ways of doing this in individual browsers such as Firefox and Explorer. In Firefox, you simply go to Edit > Preferences > General > Connection Settings and in Internet Explorer go to Internet Options > Connections > LAN Settings. There is no one way to use these tools, so experiment with these options until you achieve the desired restrictions.

There are several affordable off-the-shelf applications that can be installed and applied locally to each computer. A good list of them can be found at http://www.softplatz.com/software/restrict-Internet-access/. While some of these are more effective than others are, none of them are failsafe. Using these applications requires careful thought and then some time to implement correctly. Computer-savvy children and teens can learn how to access the control features of these applications and change them or even bypass the application all together. This is simple; if the access control is applied to one type of browser, anyone who can install software on the computer can bring in another type of browser, install it, and surf the Web unrestricted.

Many librarians know too well the troublesome task of applying restrictions to Internet access and many have simply stopped trying. Restriction software applications are either driven by keywords or are URL specific. Keyword-driven restrictions also restrict access to legitimate research sites. URL-driven restrictions need to be constantly updated as new websites are created or discovered. This takes time away from more important management of a library. Moreover, very few parents are willing to take the time to update access control lists constantly.

Most companies who allow Internet access do little to restrict access. They depend on an Internet usage policy, proactive monitoring, and applying corrective measures when necessary. Management always has the option of dismissing someone who violates written policies, and depending on how much they value the employee, that option is always available.

One family who, after trying to restrict access and then dealing with a rebellious child who kept working his way around restrictions, simply discontinued their Internet service. I'm not sure if surfing for objectionable material would warrant kicking a child out of a home, therefore the option of disconnecting from the Internet was a wise decision. The child still has a home and he has no argument about what he can see on the Internet, at least at home. For myself, I have long pondered the idea of disconnecting from the Internet at home. My local coffee shop offers free wireless access and I use the Internet so little at night after a long day of using it for business, I seriously wonder if it is worth the cost.

If that is not a viable option, contact your ISP and ask about free software they may have for restricting access. Some ISPs now even work with parents by placing content restrictions on the service they provide. School districts who want to level the playing field for their students have begun giving laptops out free of charge. Each district approaches the subject of restricting Internet access differently, and some even work directly with the local cable Internet provider in creating a service that restricts students to specific sites created or approved by the school for educational purposes only. The laptops are then configured so they can access this and only this service. This is a costly and time-consuming effort, but one these school districts believe is worth that cost.

Restricting Internet access with group policy objects is fairly easy, but may not be the best first choice for ensuring Internet safety in any given situation. There are some obvious drawbacks to this method and it does require constant updating. Consider this option carefully before implementing it. If there is going to be a fight at home with children trying to skirt around the restrictions, it may not be worth keeping the Internet access. With employees, a quick cost benefit analysis will determine how much time and effort managers want to put into developing and implementing, and then constantly updating, Internet restrictions to ensure compliance with user policies.

Chapter 31: Use Protection!
Proactive Virus and Spyware Policies

Many users have become aware of the potential risks of encountering and unknowingly downloading viruses, spyware, spybots, and rootkits, but they have not completely strategized how to protect their networking environments from them. The beginning is easy; get industry-tested antivirus software for the network and individual workstations. Schedule the updates of these applications as frequently as the manufacturer allows.

The next step is to find and install security applications that specifically focus on spybots, cookies, malware, and other types of data mining applications that do not fall into the category of a virus.

I have used Spybot Search and Destroy. It is effective at regularly scanning my hard drive for these types of applications. I also recommend doing some research on various web browsers. If you use Explorer as your default browser, go to the Microsoft website and search for information and downloads for securing Explorer. There have been known vulnerabilities and Microsoft works diligently to patch them. I recommend doing some research into Mozilla Firefox as a web browser and the companion Stopzilla, which can be configured to monitor in real time for cookies, spybots, and other types of malware. These products have proven to be fairly successful in keeping abreast with new versions of these problematic applications.

If you are managing a networked environment and choose to pay for automatic updating of antivirus protection and applications that clean spybots and cookies, prepare other users in advance to make sure their computers are able to receive the updates properly. These updates and patches are specific to threats from viruses and types of malware.

SECURITY UPDATES

Every major developer of operating systems of computer applications understands that people are constantly attempting to find vulnerabilities, and they succeed at doing so. Software applications are complex and often the need to keep the company alive by shipping product will result in missing a few of these vulnerabilities in testing. Once the product is released, updates and security patches follow as these vulnerabilities are found. Keep all operating system updates and software application updates current. This will help to limit—if not eliminate—security vulnerabilities.

Chapter 32: Minimizing Financial Transaction Risk

My father did not use the Internet. He preferred the library. Early on in my IT career, I talked with him about paying bills and banking online. After several conversations, he had a very good grasp of the essentials of networking and what the Internet was made of. He saw the potential for my generation to move wholesale into online banking and bill paying, but preferred to have my mother write a check, seal the envelope, and mail it. He saw, however, the two methods were equally risky, but that the online version might be easier to fix.

In a small town in Washington where they lived in a nice beachfront home, my parents' mail was delivered into a mailbox more than a quarter mile from the house. Walking out to get the mail was something they could do after lunch and their afternoon nap. On one occasion they had left the house in the morning and left two bills in the mailbox for the postal delivery person to pick up. They put up the small red flag, and drove away. The check was cashed days later and then the bill collector called reminding them to pay their bills. In short, someone had stolen a check from their mailbox and cashed it.

My father saw that online banking and bill paying was essentially the same thing as using a rural mail delivery system. If they were careless enough to allow the check to be intercepted, it was going to be stolen. As well, once a person had the check, they also had the account information that might allow him or her to commit further crimes in their names. From that point on, they started looking at how they could ensure security of their mail and bill paying. The results are similar to what I would recommend to anyone using online bill paying.

First, they rented a mailbox at the post office. This eliminated the possibility of someone snooping through their mailbox between the time it was delivered and the time they walked out to the road to pick it up. Second, all mail was driven into town and dropped in the secure mailbox inside the post office. Next, they did business with people and companies they knew well. If my mother bought something through the mail order catalogue, she did not buy from unknown retailers. In addition, they were wary of retailers who asked for more personal information than was required to complete the transaction. If they felt uncomfortable giving the information out, they didn't deal with the company. Finally, I was complaining to my mother about the number of email solicitations I get for bogus check fraud schemes and even more bogus charities and she showed me a pile of solicitations and charity requests she regularly gets in the mail.

The snail mail system is just as fraught with security risks as any online system and securing those transactions in a time with rising fraudulent crime requires just as much attention. Let's translate this to online transactions.

1. **Use a secure browser.** The operating system used by over 90 percent of all computers is the Windows operating system, developed by Microsoft. Their web browser, Explorer, has been cited as having security vulnerabilities, and

Microsoft has responded with upgrades and improvements to make them more secure. Do some research on Microsoft's website about these vulnerabilities and then download all updates and improvements immediately. Another browser, Firefox, has some features that are immediately more secure, but they too are constantly updating and improving their browser to ensure online security. Take the time to research these and any other browser to ensure security.

2. **Buy locally or from well-known retailers.** This good piece of advice predates the Internet by about 3,000 or so years. If you don't know the seller, understand you are taking a risk. EBay goes to great lengths to try to prevent fraud on their site, yet it happens. If I see something online I want, I determine if I can drive over to see the item and then make a decision about whether I want it. Sorry, I do not support distance purchase, nor do I have a war story about being a victim of online fraud.

3. **Read the website security and privacy policies**. I was helping a friend wade through a security and privacy policy of a site offering online banking. I discovered the webmaster's address was in Eastern Europe, the bank was "insured" by the FCID (yes, they didn't even spell it correctly), and they promised that (and the grammar really was on the site) "every transaction you makes is way secure," without

explaining the technology or processes they use to secure them. As noted previously, I have lost faith in most online retailers because when I share personal information, I get spam mails that are directly related to the inquiry I made at the original site. If I cannot complete an inquiry or a download of supposedly free information without providing personally identifying information, I give inaccurate information. The exception I make to this is websites sponsored by government agencies that require some verification of identity for admission to the site.

4. **Create and keep secret complex passwords.** I wish I would never have to repeat that statement, but I know I will for a long, long time. I listened to a radio program advising people to use pneumonic devices to remember passwords. The security guru said to take the first line of your favorite song and use the first letters of each word with a number or two thrown in. This seems like good advice on the face, but one of the methods of social engineering is precisely to discover favorite songs and bands and to begin to work with the information. There are a few different methods for selecting strong passwords that are difficult to socially engineer. There are affordable software applications for generating random passwords having no association with the user whatsoever. There are also schemes, such as spelling out the name of a randomly selected

city but using numbers and characters instead of some letters and randomly placing a special character. An example of this would be sA#kraMent0. The 'k' has the same sound as a hard 'c' and the 'O' is the really a zero. In this password I have used all four elements required for a strong password: capital letters, lowercase letters, numbers, and special characters. Not only is it going to be difficult to guess, but password cracking software will not easily or quickly reveal this password.

5. **Do not give out any optional information**. The more information you give, the more personally identifiable you are and the easier it will be to socially engineer your passwords or to steal your identity.

6. **Do not save credit card information on to a website even if prompted to do so**. This upsets a very large online retailer located in Seattle. I no longer buy from them because they automatically saved my credit card information to their "secure" servers and keep a log of all my search, review, and purchase activity.

7. **Print a record of the terms and the actual transaction.** Many people are overcharged when purchasing online. Keeping track of all agreed upon terms and the actual transaction does not eliminate the hassle, but it helps when there is a problem, and these hassles are easier to deal with if you are fully prepared for them.

8. **Know and test the refund policies.** A wise Internet shopper occasionally buys gifts he or she never intends to give just to return them and test the refund policy. Read and understand the policy before testing it; you may not get money back, but have to take store credit instead.

Online transactions should be absolutely secure, but then even when I bought a vacuum cleaner from a small-town, church-going salesman who promised me total money-back satisfaction, I went back to buy bags for it a week later and he was out of business and long gone. These are the basic steps to take to ensure security. From here, you simply need to apply some common sense.

Chapter 33: Preventing Identity Theft, Chat-Sniffing, Cyber-Stalking, and Bullying

The guy who responded to a seemingly personal email from the Secretary of Finance of an African country is not urban legend. He was lured into a scam where he needed to "finance" the transition of millions of dollars from offshore accounts to his account and he was guaranteed the millions of dollars in interest and finder's fees for his generous efforts. Of course, the $35,000 he fronted for the "financing" end of the bargain disappeared and the whole thing was a scam. There has been more than one victim of this.

Understanding why people want your personal information will help you determine the best methods for preventing theft. There are predators who want information about children or adults so they can stalk and abuse them. There are laws that prevent websites from even allowing children to identify themselves. Adults can identify anything they like about themselves for all to read. Also, social security numbers, birthdates, addresses, job titles, and other types of personal financial information are easily used to secure credit cards, loans, and other types of financial service. At one company, a highly trusted receptionist was arrested for using this kind of information from 16 employees to illegally acquire credit cards that he used to pay off other credit cards. Finally, given the proper amount of information, a person could use your identity to conduct illicit or illegal activity on a computer. Spoofing techniques, when properly applied, can even make it appear as if the perpetrator used your computer.

Instant messaging is a common Internet activity that yields the best quality personal identity information for potential thieves. Users of messenger services are advised when they install and configure these applications not to include information such as bank account and social security numbers in the messages. This information can be seen by anyone with a cheap chat-sniffing software application. Many companies and organizations block and uninstall messenger services for this and other security reasons. Many user policies are explicit in not allowing the use of messenger services, especially in grade schools.

Messenger services use a protocol that exchanges information in plain text, as if you were writing a message in Notepad or some other plain text application. These patterns of ones and zeros are easily intercepted and reproduced by anyone with the sniffing software.

A security assessment of a bank in the Seattle area pinpointed the cause of huge information leaks regarding customer account information; bankers were chatting internally and externally with staff and customers putting names, addresses, account numbers, dollar figures, and even social security numbers in these chat sessions. The use of instant messaging was banned immediately.

Finally, knowing who is reading your blog, chat sessions, and email will help reduce the theft of personal information. Unwittingly, even children who contribute to these types of online forums include information about themselves that would allow a predator to identify and locate them. This might be perfectly acceptable, but in many cases it is not. Friendship web portals where students identify themselves in association with their school can and has led to stalking.

The Internet and the tools developed for communicating there are a double-edged sword. They allow for immediate and effective communication and introductions between people who might otherwise never meet. Knowing who and where you are can lead to stealing personal information or heaping abuse on you as a victim of stalking or bullying. The action items that follow will help prevent the loss or abuse of personal information. Let's focus on action items to help prevent abuse or theft of personal data by mitigation of membership; information; instant messaging; social engineering; and cyber identity.

MEMBERSHIP INFORMATION

I am not an advocate of lying when creating user profiles for email and web portals. There is usually the option of not adding information such as a real name, address, age, or anything else the portal requests. A clever moniker with no photograph or any other personal information usually allows the user to proceed and enjoy the benefits of the cyber community. If this is not an option, consider the value of membership against the potential of abuse of personal information. Most free email, dating, or social cyber communities will allow anonymous membership with the option of adding more information later by updating a profile.

The use of professional cyber communities to gain access to research materials often requires the member to identify many aspects of his or her profession clearly, even salary range. The member gets free access to valuable information at the expense of completing extensive personal profiles. I have declined most of these especially when they request information about my age, salary, job title, company, and level of education. In spite of promises, the information is for their edification only, I am aware of the market for demographic information that is sold to spamming professionals. Many other information technology professionals openly admit to lying in these profiles just to get the information without giving away valuable personal and professional information.

Take the time to view the personal profile for every email address, cyber community membership, and chat room you belong to. Remove or conceal any information you would not want a stranger to know.

INSTANT MESSAGING

Third-party applications can be purchased to encrypt instant messaging. Most of them require both parties to have the same application. This is a strategy deployed by some companies; instant messaging would then be allowed within the confines of the company because no outsider would have legitimate access to the corporate licensing and would therefore not have the software and configurations needed to decrypt the messages.

If encrypting messages is not a practical solution, continue using instant messaging as if you are having a conversation with someone in a room full of strangers who can hear and copy every word. This same principle applies to chat rooms, discussion forums, and any other type of real-time exchange of cyber information. It is also important to remember when using chat rooms. Certain kinds of information exchange can be considered criminal activity, such as making threats on the life of another person. Every word contributed to the chat room is preserved. It might be difficult, but rarely impossible, to identify the person contributing illegal content to a chat session.

SOCIAL ENGINEERING
When someone overhears a conversation in a coffee shop and jots down personal identifiers, this is not yet illegal. What they do with the information might be. This is a very pernicious form of social engineering. There was an expression during World War II that was used to caution people not to talk about where their loved ones were located, "Loose Lips Sink Ships." Keep this in mind when discussing passwords, account information, and anything else that someone could use.

When I was an administrator in a private school, one of the instructors had the ability to watch my hands as I typed a very complex password to gain administrative access. I was not aware he was watching and later caught him managing a workstation after entering the password. I now always ask people to turn away as I type in any password. Many administrators, myself among them, become suspicious of anyone acting too kindly and asking for information about the network he or she otherwise should not have. I simply smile and tell him or her not to take it personally; when it comes to data security I trust no one.

During routine internal audits in a major corporation, the auditor would ask for keys that would give him unrestricted access to all staff level workstations. In spite of numerous warnings, the auditor would inevitably find log in names and passwords written on scraps of paper and either hidden under the keyboard or pinned to a bulletin board by the workstation. Imagine the fun one could have with someone else's access. Educate personnel on the risks of poor password management; anyone with after-hour access to the workstation can log on as that person and gain access to personal or company data or conduct illicit and illegal activity on the Internet under the name of the person who left his or her password lying around.

ASSESSING CYBER IDENTITIES

Try a few common methods used to capture personal information from the Internet. Launch your web browser and use whatever search engine you prefer. Google is good, but there are other engines that will produce different results. In the search engine, type your full name. My search usually results in about 20 links that contain information about my books, my employer, my work as a board member for a charitable organization, and even a link to a short story I wrote. People I lost track of over the years have used this method to find me. They were able to ascertain my employer, get my email address, and even discovered through news articles about my books where I would be appearing for a book singing. One person, whom

I like and respect, showed up at the signing in order to renew a long lost friendship.

Fortunately, when I search my own name I do not find any derogatory information. While assisting others, however, this was not the case. People of every age are vulnerable to negative, libelous statements that someone might post in a cyber-community or on a website.

Cyber bullies target teenage peers using this tactic, creating horrific lies about the victim, and letting anyone who cares read the forum, chat room, or blog postings. These postings are frequently available through search engines. It is common now for teenagers to advertise what they have posted about their victims and encourage other peers to access the sites and read the damaging information or view an embarrassing photograph.

If you find false and negative information on a website, contact the webmaster immediately. There is a contact link for every webmaster. If you find false and negative information on a social cyber-community, contact the manager for that site immediately. In both cases, demand that the information be removed. By law, they must remove the negative information until the poster can prove the information is of public record, such as a criminal or civil judgment.

If you are a victim of cyber bullying or if an adult tries to have a conversation about sexual activity with children you know or if you experience any other kind of exchange of information that could be considered illegal, report the activity immediately to your local police authorities. Do not respond to the abuser unless specifically instructed to do so by the police.

It is worth noting in this chapter the concept of proper preservation of evidence. Take a course sometime from a community college offering degrees in criminal justice on cyber-evidence or invite local law enforcement to speak to a group about preserving evidence. It will help you assist the police capture and convict those who choose to steal your identity or to conduct illegal activity on the Internet. Do not ever try to police the Internet yourself; you will only help the perpetrators.

Chapter 34: The National Industrial Security Program; A Comprehensive Security Model

The National Industrial Security Program serves as a complete and easy-to-understand model for a security program. To ensure the right people manage the secret information assets belonging to the Department of Defense but are sitting on servers belonging to private contractors, the DoD has written specific guidelines for the safe keeping of that information. Used primarily to serve as a security model for civilian subcontractors to the Department of Defense, it is useful to examine because of its completeness and simplicity.

The document known as the *National Industrial Security Program Operations Manual* (NISPOM) defines, in detail, the levels of security for employees to determine levels of access as well as the criteria for being certified to house these varying levels of secret information and conduct business with the various agencies of the DoD. It goes on further to define processes and policies necessary for securing these systems.

The focus of the first section of this chapter will be to highlight the important issues necessary to attain the proper level of certification in order to contract with the DoD.

The second section will serve as an overview of the specific security requirements contained in this document. There has been some confusion about conflicting available copies of the NISPOM, and the supplemental copy produced in 2004 acknowledges that chapter 8 on

(Information Security) was written in 1998, and as of that date, had not been updated. The DoD released a revised version in February of 2006. This is the version used for my purposes here. This chapter is an interpretation of the document and the process geared for the home or small business. Contractors who live under the NISP tell me the terms can be interpreted differently on a case by case basis by representatives of the DoD. This chapter then serves as a general overview of the intent and applicability of specific security issues covered in this book and I do not represent this to be an official interpretation of the exact terms a contractor would need to satisfy in order to obtain certification.

Also, any reference to the DoD Orange Book comes with the same caveat. While the Orange Book has been the de facto standard for information security within the DoD, versions that are available to the general public are outdated. Only fully cleared military personnel have access to the official documents. The mention of the Orange Book here is referential only and does not intend to be an official interpretation.

CERTIFICATION

Section 2 of chapter 8 of the NISPOM gives a clear picture of what is required to obtain certification. It begins with a clarification that the security measures must be in place and then certified. While there are provisions for certifying subsequent measures that are in progress under the initial certification, the systems must be designed and all security measures in place before the certificate will be issued.

246

There has been some confusion with contractors on this. The operating manual, however, is clear.

The operating manual is also clear that the security measures may be tested onsite before certification is issued. This helps the certifying body determine if the system is built to accommodate and support an acceptable level of risk. That level of risk is decided by the certifying body, not the contractor. Before any classified information can sit on the server and be accessed by approved contractual personnel, this determination must be made in advance.

There is a provision to grant interim approval, but this is decided by the certifying body and the manual is clear that the security measures must be in place for the first 180 days of provisional certification, and then for the possible 180-day extension. The process of reaccreditation must be completed whenever the contractor substantially changes their security processes or upgrades their infrastructure. The IS security manager (ISSM) determines if the changes warrant a review by the certifying body and they are solely responsible for determining if reaccreditation is necessary.

The certifying body can revoke the certificate if specific security measures are removed, fail, or are altered so as not to provide the acceptable level of risk. The system is then sanitized and all classified information is removed.

In the event the contractor wishes to certify multiple systems, he or she is required to submit a master system security plan (Master SSP). Once the first system is certified under the plan, all subsequent systems are certified only when they meet the acceptable level of risk. A thorough risk assessment is conducted by the certifying body with the assistance of approved contractor personnel. While there might be several readers of this book interested in eventually doing business with the DoD and will need more detailed information about certification, most will not and this is all we need to know about the certification process for our purposes here.

COMMON REQUIREMENTS

Section 3 of chapter 8 lists the requirements for securing systems and they are lengthy and comprehensive. The reader will identify with the topics already covered in this book.

Clearing and Sanitizing

The intent of this section is to either totally remove classified information from a system, such as in the case of loss of certification, or to reuse the media. In the case of media reuse, it is cleared to prevent access to the information that was stored there. Sanitizing is a lower level of data removal. The specific guidelines for clearing and sanitizing are the province of the certifying body and issued to the contractor. One thing is very clear; sanitize only that which you will never need again.

Examination of Software and Hardware

The certifying body will examine all commercial or proprietary software to ascertain if there are bugs, viruses, incompatibilities, or anything else that might be considered detrimental to the security of the classified information. Hardware is also examined to ensure that it is in good working order and does not present a security risk. Why not apply this same principle to a home or small business network as well? I would add to this examination a thorough review of all software licenses.

Identification and Authentication Management
This is, for obvious reasons, one of the most extensively detailed parts of the chapter covering IS security. How people log on, how their user profiles are managed, the development of passwords, the removal of users, and the reuse of log in IDs are meticulously covered. The chapters in authentication, password management, and access controls in this book are a good guideline for meeting these standards. Of particular interest in this section is the standard for password generation and management. The certifying body will define how passwords are generated and where they are stored. Writing them down on a sticky note and placing them under the keyboard is absolutely not acceptable. Again, the DoD requires a comprehensive plan for complex authentication; why not apply the same principle to any other network?

Maintenance
The NISPOM recognizes my long-held belief that a system is extremely vulnerable during both routine and unscheduled maintenance. There are two tiers of personnel allowed to conduct maintenance; cleared and uncleared. Cleared personnel do not require an escort, but uncleared personnel not only require appropriately cleared personnel to escort them, but they will also be subject to keystroke monitoring. Uncleared personnel will not have any access

to classified data even while being escorted and monitored. Their role is hardware maintenance only. This may be a little overkill for a home network, but definitely merits consideration for a small business network housing very valuable proprietary information.

Malicious Code

The standards established in earlier chapters of this book are to be met with regard to constantly monitoring for any malicious codes and the download of necessary security patches to the operating system. This is a constant effort that if routinely scheduled and implemented is easier than flossing your teeth and goes a long way toward permanently securing any networked system.

Physical Security

The standard here is not only the use of locks and cameras to observe the physical space, but the uses of access logs to data bases and security devices placed on hardware. The hardware will also be supported with alternate power supplies and surge/suppress protection to ensure the integrity and availability of the data on the hardware. One small company in San Diego asked if I would serve as a security consultant to evaluate their system as they sought certification required by the DoD. I walked into the public area of their office and discovered the server was housed behind a receptionist desk and I waited in that area for 15 minutes for any human being to show up and ask what I needed. Knowing how lax their security was, I walked away from the opportunity. It was obvious they did not grasp even the most fundamental concept of physical security.

Review of Output and Media

The classified information stored on the system is to remain classified even when hard copy or electronic copy stored on portable media is required. This is not a high standard to maintain for any system. The certifying body will determine all necessary clearance procedures for the production and distribution of the information that passes from the information system to an area outside of the protected zone.

Configuration Management

The intent here has been thoroughly covered in this book; assess and catalogue all hardware and software, determine reliability of connectivity, determine the sensitivity of ports and hardware, and then document this in a configuration management plan. Following any catastrophic failure of a system, the system can be rebuilt to original specs quickly and the data backups can be deployed, minimizing down time.

Protection Measures

Section 4 of chapter 8 of the NISPOM defines levels of protection measures for varying types of data. The matrices in this section define sensitivity for the confidentiality, integrity, and availability of data. The three levels are high, medium, and basic for each. Confidential information can be classified top secret and secret, or secret and secret restricted, and then simply confidential. For the integrity of

251

the data, the three levels are absolute accuracy, high degree of accuracy, and then a reasonable degree of accuracy. The availability of data is determined by immediately available on demand, readily available, and then available with a flexible tolerance for delay.

These standards are then tested against clearance matrices and then against the various standards of the operating manual. Once these matrices are understood, it becomes clear that the operating manual sets a clear standard for protecting classified information but also allows for normal operations for lower or nonclassified data. One former contractor complained his operations were unduly restricted by the standards in the operating manual, but he also admitted he tried to secure everything and did not utilize the lower levels of acceptable confidentiality, integrity, and availability allowed. In a small business, if this is thought through and implemented carefully, segmenting users in some hierarchical manner will immediately reduce the risk of inappropriate or malicious access to data.

Protection Requirements
Section 6 of chapter 8 of the NISPOM defines protection requirements. This includes alternate power supplies, auditing capability, backup and restoration procedures, changes to data that affect integrity, data transmission, access controls, identification and authentication, separation of functions, system recovery, and disaster recovery planning.

The *National Industrial Security Program Operating Manual* is based on solid, proven security measures that should apply to any sensitive data. While the research and development of the tools necessary for national security are extremely important, so is data pertaining to the finances and trade secrets of corporations and my personal data.

Beginning with a basic understanding of networking and the transmission of data, we have carefully followed these rigid standards throughout this book and seen how these standards are necessary for securing these types of data.

The sad reality is that outside of contractors working on national security, too many people fail to educate themselves on these issues and how simple they are to implement. Therefore, sensitive data goes unprotected. Fortunately, lawmakers are catching up with laws governing the security of financial, health, and personal data.

CASE STUDY: NISP OPERATING MANUAL CH 8 APPLIED

I have been associated with a small research and development firm that has taken on mostly academic research into applying alternate materials to explore the possibilities of conducting electricity through unseen channels of conductivity. This same research, with a radically different application, caught the eye of a defense contractor. I can say their desired outcome has nothing to do with electrical conductivity, but I cannot say what it is focused on because I simply do not know. They have never revealed that to me. What I do know is that their computer systems were not well maintained or secured and the owners of the R&D firm set out to change that.

It wasn't necessarily the possibility of becoming a subcontractor for defense research that triggered this, but it helped. The principles realized that even an amateur could access their data. They had no security policy, no security perimeter, and no software to detect viruses, spybots, and worms. Nor did they have any malware. In a brief and monitored penetration test, I simply showed them how anyone could ping their IP address and scan for open ports, and I explained what could happen from there.

Their response was classic. They simply did not know anything about these potential threats nor had they taken any time to determine how vulnerable they were. They also had no budget for any professional information technology personnel and relied on technical hobbyists to maintain their systems. After taking a preliminary view of their network and talking to their employees (who "duct taped" their system together) and then having shown them the most minimal penetration test possible, I declined to be associated with their network and the protection of proprietary data. I left with a warning that prior to taking on any defense subcontracting, they needed to fix the problem. I introduced them to the model presented here and I left.

Two years later, during the updating of material for this book, I was approached to give an analysis of their progress. To date they have not taken on any defense subcontracting; they decided instead to get their IT house in order prior to bidding on any work. As a patriot and an IT professional, I applaud their decision.

They have invested not only in hardware and software that will serve as a foundation for a strong perimeter but they have also written and adopted a security policy that is audited once a year by an independent third party. They adopted the standards in the *NISP Operating Manual* and, except for a few issues, now have a system that is fairly well protected both from outside attacks as well as from the inside. Of particular note, they have paid for training for three employees to architect, manage, and secure their network and they rotate the administrative duties. No one employee, except for the owners, will ever have exclusive control. They update the security patches on all local computers as well as the server, and the server room is locked and air-conditioned. I liked the architecture of their data storage, and agreed not to give any specifics about that.   I also agreed not to give any specific information here about their authentication procedures or their encryption methods. Nevertheless, I can nod my approval.

It has taken two years for them to get here and they admitted my refusal to consult them, and subsequently take on some level of responsibility for the security of their data, was the wake-up call. They admitted freely investing in information security to a recognized standard was less expensive than losing proprietary research data and then, most likely, any possibility of staying in business.

Conclusion: A Call to Action

I accept that we need to protect children using the Internet. Sometimes we need to help with the overt trustworthiness of the elderly who can be easily conned and scammed. What I am hoping to also make clear is the rest of us might need to save us from ourselves. My generation created the Internet the way it is. Few could predict how potentially dangerous the Internet would become. We foresaw some of the nefarious activity, but certainly not to the extent we see it today. Perhaps this is a byproduct of freedom.

Just to reflect for a minute, it is my generation that heralded the personal computer and subsequent generations were raised with them until now they are a ubiquitous figure in every home. It is my generation that wrote the program that sends spam, and the following generations use it. It is my generation that invented data mining, and former students of mine use that every day. My generation, perhaps funded by a few members of the previous generation, discovered Internet pornography is a multibillion dollar business and we made those websites available to anyone with an Internet connection. I don't see the X or Y generations taking these sites down.

My generation also created an Internet with 10 billion web pages containing information about virtually anything. I can book a flight while I am lying in bed. I can look up restaurants in my city. I can find papers on nanotechnology and the most current theories of Hemingway's novels. I can listen to my favorite radio stations in other cities and watch video of politicians making huge verbal mistakes by insulting people, not thinking their words would find their way to a video share site.

For the most part, the Internet is a place where adults behave in a legal manner as adults. In many ways, much of this behavior can be considered offensive, but these are within their rights act as they do. Our society has responded with laws protecting children especially, but instead of always resorting to new regulations and control, we need to begin a long discussion not only in this country, but the world over on the power of the Internet and the responsibility we have to use this power wisely.

Under the guise of protection, large corporations seek to gain control of the very heart of the Internet in a manner that will seemingly regulate content, but will really regulate access. Losing our freedom of speech because a few people will wreak havoc with this tool is not worth it. I like the freedom of speech I enjoy on the Internet and I have no intention of allowing corporations or governments to take that away for any reason.

It's not enough to focus this book on being wary of bogus check-cashing schemes and virus infections from seemingly innocent websites. I have pointed out many strategies and practical actions we can take to protect ourselves. Rather than putting on blinders or simply using passive protections, we need to be proactive in our efforts to make our home and small business computing secure and safe.

I run a spybot remover on a laptop I intentionally take off my home fire wall for research purposes. I found five copies of a popular key-logger software application loaded on to my computer. I went to the website for this product and read the glowing ad copy about how terrific it was, how parents could record everything their kids do on the Internet. The problem is, this same application is perniciously loaded on to unsuspecting computers and the owner doesn't know about it. I could not figure out where the key-logging data was being sent, so I removed all copies instead. I notified their customer support about the incident and they sent me auto response emails telling me how terrific the product is and it is "best of breed." I fully accept these intrusions in a controlled environment for research purposes, but I am saddened that I need to continuously monitor ever more powerful and pernicious activity.

Computer security and Internet safety begin with a commitment to responsible use. This goes for both the passive user as well as the content provider. In addition to the preventive measures I laid out in this book, I further suggest taking a few steps outside of the realm of your personal network toward a safer and more secure computing environment.

First, avoid the obviously risky activity on the Internet. Using common sense and many of the suggestions in this book, you can live like the man I know. He claims he does not go out to buy anything except groceries and gas and he has never been scammed or lost his financial identity, ever. I asked him his methodology for buying online and almost word for word he recited back to me the information in chapter 18. The message is simple; avoid the risk. He goes to extreme measures that may not always be necessary, but the sentiment of thinking about and researching the risk is now an essential activity.

Second, let companies know you do not want their spam and do not give out information that would reveal your identity. Let your voice be heard; you will not tolerate their activity and if they persist you will avoid their products. Associates in the IT world brag often about how they turn these unsolicited emails into denial of service attacks or spam bombs, and this is simply illegal. Don't do to them what they do to you. If I am the only person demanding my information be kept private, they will only laugh, but if collectively users want to act to keep their online transactions and data private, they will probably move on to some other pernicious method of flooding our lives with useless information and gaining access to personal information. A good place to start is the social networks who introduce new features continuously with the sole intent of accessing more of your personal data. Tell them to stop.

As we examined the technical infrastructure of the Internet in the first section of this book, I wanted to point out how easy it is to provide information and how this information is available to anyone with an Internet connection. I would never want to curtail the freedoms we enjoy on the Internet; I am only advocating action on the part of the users who want to take control of their privacy. Not using a product sends a clear message to the company making the product: We don't like what you are doing.

The final response I advocate is proactively challenging lies that are placed on the Internet. I read several blogs of persons I trust. One writer was viciously attacked on a website for no apparent reason. Collectively, the readers of the blog challenged the lies placed on the offending website asking for proof. Eventually, the writer of the lies took the information down, however, without apology. In a more notable case, a 12-year-old boy was asked to respond to remarks made by the President of the United States on the S-CHIP program that provided medical coverage to families in a specific income bracket. Several websites intentionally posted lies regarding the financial worth of the family and questioned their need for any assistance. The lies were quickly challenged and ultimately removed.

In the case of the 12-year-old boy, one website wrote inflammatory lies and published the family's address. I saw this and immediately expressed my concern to the webmaster of the site for the safety of that family. Making a political point in a free society had crossed the lines into creating an unsafe environment for children. The only possible response to that is a challenge to the lies and threats created by such statements.

It is easier to use the Internet as a bully pulpit and make any kind of statement you like, no matter how false or threatening. It requires individuals to report threats, challenge lies, and otherwise tell the source of this kind of information their behavior is unacceptable.

I wish there were no threats to your private data or to your person on the Internet, but that is not the case. We are vulnerable whenever we log on. It's not enough to simply be aware of the threats and to take passive action to protect ourselves. This is the least effective protection. It is also not acceptable to undertake any illegal retaliation against a company or individual. What is left is a proactive and responsible approach to identifying spammers, data miners, identity thieves, predators, and liars and to expose or publicly challenge their offending behavior. Happy and safe computing!

About the Author

Shawn Rohrbach has spent the past twenty years working in networked computing focusing on migration to enterprise technologies with particular attention paid to security issues. He holds an MBA in Information Systems from City University in Bellevue, Washington and an MFA in writing from Naropa University in Boulder, Colorado. He is currently serving as an Information Technology Consultant to San Diego State University. Prior to this position, he spent ten years serving as Associate Dean of Information Technology for ITT Technical Institute in Everett, Washington. Shawn volunteers some time each month to teach internet security methods to home schooling families.

Author Websites

Author Site
www.shawnrohrbach.com

Information Security Blog
http://it.toolbox.com/blogs/cover-your-assets/

For more about our books,
please visit:

www.AuthorMikeInk.com